LIVING
the
HEIDELBERG

The Heidelberg Catechism and the Moral Life

by
ALLEN VERHEY

CRC Publications
Grand Rapids, Michigan

FOR RICHARD AND CATHERINE VERHEY

© 1986 by CRC Publications, 2850 Kalamazoo Avenue SE, Grand Rapids, Michigan 49560. All rights reserved. Printed in the United States of America.

Library of Congress Cataloging-in-Publication Data

Verhey, Allen.
  Living the Heidelberg.

  Bibliography: p.
  1. Heidelberger Katechismus. I. Title.
BX9428.V46   1986   238'.42   85–31386
ISBN 0-903265-21-1 (pbk.)

Contents

PREFACE

THE HEIDELBERG CATECHISM is a major confessional statement of the Reformed/Presbyterian family of churches; it ranks with the Westminster Catechism as a sourcebook for instruction in the faith, following the Calvinistic tradition. But the Heidelberg (as it is affectionately called) functions far deeper in the churches that hold to it: its Lord's Days pattern preaching, its language permeates prayers, its phrases fill sermons, and its answers frame the living faith of believers.

Given that central role, it's not surprising that some question what this sixteenth-century document has to say to modern Calvinists about the social-ethical issues raised by our changing, multiracial, multiform society. In this study, Dr. Verhey answers that question. He contends that the catechism has clear social and ethical implications, that it speaks unequivocally to many of the social justice issues of our day.

The Rev. Dr. Allen Verhey is a minister of the Christian Reformed Church, presently Assistant Professor of Religion at Hope College, Holland, Michigan. An earlier version of this study, commissioned by the Synodical Committee on Race Relations of the Christian Reformed Church, was published in a series of articles in THE BANNER, March–September, 1979.

This book is intended not only for pastors who preach on the Heidelberger; informed lay people, for whom the catechism is the most intimate expression of faith, also should welcome this guide to living the catechism they confess.

Harvey A. Smit
Director of Education

1

CONFESSION AND AGENDA

THE HEIDELBERG CATECHISM —I memorized it as a growing boy at the insistence of my parents. I still remember struggling to recall the words without fully understanding them, usually failing my father's initial oral examination, but always receiving his praise when I finally got it right. The sessions were sometimes tedious then, but I look back on them now with a certain fondness. I can remember my father admonishing me, "And now remember, son, it's not enough just to memorize these words. You must take them to heart and try to live them."

"To live them"—that sounded like strange advice to me then. But it is that advice which this book wants to repeat and develop.

The connection between doctrine and life that my father insisted on and this book attempts to develop is not, of course, my family's invention. The Heidelberg Catechism itself makes the same point. Already in question and answer 1 it promises that the comfort of which it speaks will make us "wholeheartedly willing and ready from now on to live for him" (Q & A 1).

From the very beginning of the catechism, then, it is clear that the section on the Christian life of gratitude is no mere addendum or supplement to Christian doctrine. My father admonished me as he did because he had already learned his catechism well. It's not enough just to memorize these words; they must enter our hearts and also our lives, making us "whole-heartedly willing and ready from now on to live for him."

If my father was echoing the Heidelberg Catechism with his advice, the catechism was echoing its spiritual father, John Calvin, who had

5

earlier insisted that doctrine never be divorced from life nor life from doctrine.

> *It is a doctrine not of the tongue but of life. It is not apprehended by the understanding and memory alone, as other disciplines are, but it is received only when it possesses the whole soul, and finds a seat and resting place in the inmost affection of the heart. . . . it must enter our heart and pass into our daily living, and so transform us into itself that it may not be unfruitful for us.*
>
> —Institutes, *3, vi, 4*

So John Calvin spoke about Christian conviction. At this point and at many others the catechism stands in the tradition of this great reformer. And from time to time this book will look to Calvin in its attempt better to understand the catechism and its implications for life today.

For all the spiritual kinship between the catechism and John Calvin, however, it was doubtless more important to the writers of the catechism that Scripture itself discloses as falsehood the divorce of faith from practice, of conviction from decision and action. Probably no one spoke more sharply against a "faith" irrelevant to decision and action than James did (see James 2:14–26), but throughout the Scriptures—in the law, the Prophets, Wisdom, the Gospels, the Epistles—faith in the God of Abraham, Isaac, and Jacob, loyalty to the God who raised Jesus from death, is a matter of life, not merely of tongue. The whole Bible agrees with James that we must "be doers of the word" (James 1:22). It is on Scripture that the catechism finally rests, and any attempt to understand and live the catechism in today's world will be constrained to turn and return to the same Scripture.

The intention of this little book is to understand the Heidelberg Catechism in the light of our contemporary social responsibilities and to try to understand our contemporary social responsibilities in the light of the catechism. It will hold fast to the connection between doctrine and life and, with the help of John Calvin and the Scripture, attempt to understand what living the Heidelberg Catechism means in a world like this one.

It is important for the reader to know that the lad who memorized the catechism at the insistence of his parents grew up to confess it and to become a member (and minister) of the Christian Reformed Church, a confessional church for whom the catechism is "a doctrinal standard." The catechism is my creed and confession—and my church's. This book, then, does not approach the catechism merely as a sixteenth-century document, but rather as "a living document," a living instrument in the teaching and preaching of the church. The focus is not merely historical; rather, the focus is on the continuing comfort and challenge that come to the church through fresh readings and rereadings of her confessions.

Of course, we may not deny that the catechism is a sixteenth-century document. It does not (and could not) directly address contemporary social questions. The sixteenth century was not the twentieth, after all. But in spite of its age, this sixteenth-century document remains relevant to

6

our life as a community of God's people in and for the world. It is my conviction that the catechism has illumined and can continue to illumine the church's attempts to be faithful—not only in doctrine but in life. Indeed, to state again that link between doctrine and life on which my father, the catechism, John Calvin, and Scripture have always insisted, if we own the catechism as "a doctrinal standard," then we must follow its passage from doctrine to life. We must allow the catechism to form and inform our intentions, our attitudes, and our perspectives—including our social intentions, our social attitudes, and our social perspectives.

Some have claimed, however, that the catechism has no interest in a social ethic. George W. Richards, for example, charges that the catechism is "individualistic and other-worldly." It is important to say candidly at the very beginning that I disagree radically with that charge. I do not deny that the catechism is written in a warm, personal, and experiential way, and I do not claim that the sixteenth century was the twentieth. But I do deny that the catechism is "individualistic and other-worldly," and I do assert its interest in the social morality of the sixteenth century (Q. 110 with its references to merchandising, counterfeiting, and usury is an obvious example) and its relevance to the social morality of the twentieth century.

The warmth of the catechism has been one of its great strengths and has helped it find "a seat and resting place in the inmost affection of the heart." Yet that strength can also be a weakness if it tempts us to hear the catechism merely as an address to an introspective and individualistic conscience, to a conscience that looks only inward and is concerned only with the relationship of one's inner self with God. If we succumb to that temptation, then we do not genuinely hear or understand the catechism.

The warmth and piety of the catechism do not serve as retreats from cold, secular life. On the contrary, this confession is "a handbook of practical religion" (so stated the foreword to the 400th anniversary edition). The catechism never forgets the neighbor. It never becomes individualistic. It affirms what might be called "the triadic structure" of the Christian life—that is, that we are always at once related to both God and our neighbors and must see our neighbors as persons related to both God and ourselves. So to genuinely hear and understand the catechism, we must be prepared to have it address our social consciences and our social situation. We must allow it, along with the Scriptures, to form and inform a social conscience in the churches.

Those are the convictions that have shaped and will guide this book. It is not the book's intention to say the last word about either the catechism or social ethics. The intention is rather simply to contribute to the moral discourse and discernment that occur within the Christian community—and particularly of those communities within which the catechism is confessed.

Subsequent chapters survey the catechism. Chapter 2 deals with the famous first question and answer, identifying and explicating the social relevance of some of its major themes, and concludes with a concrete example of the relevance of the catechism to investments.

Chapter 3 discusses questions 4 and 5, the catechism's demand of love and its realism about human sin. The chapter traces some of the general social and political implications of the catechism here, and concludes with some concrete applications of love in a world of selfishness.

Chapter 4 sweeps more broadly, touching on questions 6–19, the fall and God's deliverance. The chapter develops the social implications of our responsibility to God the creator, judge, and deliverer, and concludes with a consideration of the relevance of such responsibility to race relations.

Chapter 5 concentrates on questions 26–28, explicating the moral significance of the catechism's statements on creation and providence, and applying them concretely to ecology.

Chapter 6 focuses on the catechism's confession in questions 29–34 that Jesus Christ is Lord, identifying some of the socially significant themes related to this confession. The chapter develops particularly the theme of liberation, attempting to relate it in a final section to contemporary movements for liberation.

Chapter 7 focuses on our membership in Christ, a matter addressed by questions 32–90 of the catechism. The chapter concentrates on the moral significance of our participation in Christ, concluding with an analysis of the church as a community of moral discourse and discernment.

Chapters 8 and 9 are straightforward commentary on questions 93–114, the catechisms's handling of the Ten Commandments. The Commandments, and the catechism's treatment of them, remain morally relevant and full of concrete implications for our social life in the twentieth century.

Chapter 10, finally, deals with the catechism's treatment of the Lord's Prayer, develops the social significance of this prayer, and imitates the catechism by ending its commentary not only on prayer but with prayers.

Much, the reader can see, has been dared. This book is not quite a commentary on the catechism, not quite a treatise on social ethics. It is an attempt to confess the catechism in today's world and to insist that we have the courage to move from confession to agenda—that is, to what is to be done. It is given by one member of a community "for the service and enrichment of the other members" (Q & A 55). It is not given as the last word, but as a helpful word. It is meant to encourage the churches to think, talk, and pray about their social responsibilities in the light of their confession of the catechism.

It is in the churches, not on these pages, that the confession of the catechism can "pass into our daily living, and so transform us into itself that it may not be unfruitful for us" nor we for the world. It is there, not on these pages, that the comfort of the catechism can make us "whole-heartedly willing and ready from now on to live for him."

Acknowledgments and Suggestions for Further Reading

Throughout this book references to Scripture are to the Revised Standard Version. Richard Mouw's fine book *Politics and the Biblical Drama* (Grand Rapids: Wm. B. Eerdmans, 1976) provides a rich and readable resource on the bearing of Scripture on questions of social responsibility. See also Allen Verhey, *The Great Reversal: The New Testament and Ethics* (Grand Rapids: Wm. B. Eerdmans, 1984).

The references to Calvin's *Institutes* are quoted from *Calvin: Institutes of the Christian Religion*, edited by John T. McNeill, translated by Ford Lewis Battles (Philadelphia: The Westminster Press, 1960; *Library of Christian Classics*, Vols. XX and XXI). The little book by Andre Bieler, *The Social Humanism of Calvin*, translated by Paul T. Fuhrmann (Richmond: John Knox Press, 1964), is still a good introduction to the social thought of Calvin. One may also consult W. Fred Graham, *The Constructive Revolutionary: John Calvin and his Socio-Economic Impact* (Richmond: John Knox Press, 1971).

On the relation between doctrine and life I recommend the excellent article by G.C. Berkouwer, "Orthodoxy and Orthopraxis" in *God and the Good: Essays in Honor of Henry Stob*, edited by C. Orlebeke and L. Smedes (Grand Rapids: Wm. B. Eerdmans, 1975).

Chapter 1 cited these books on the catechism: George W. Richards, *The Heidelberg Catechism: Historical and Doctrinal Studies* (Philadelphia: Publication and Sunday School Board of the Reformed Church in the United States, 1913), page 118; and *The Heidelberg Catechism with Commentary: 400th Anniversary Edition 1563–1963* (New York: Pilgrim Press, 1963), page 7.

The reader may also want to consult these additional works on the catechism: Karl Barth, *The Heidelberg Catechism for Today* (Richmond: John Knox Press, 1964); Henry Stob, "The Heidelberg Catechism in Moral Perspective," *Ethical Reflections: Essays on Moral Themes* (Grand Rapids: Wm. B. Eerdmans, 1978); Howard Hageman, "The Catechism in Christian Nurture," in Bard Thompson et al., *Essays on the Heidelberg Catechism* (Philadelphia: United Church Press, 1963); Donald J. Bruggink, ed., *Guilt, Grace and Gratitude* (New York: The Half Moon Press, 1963).

The phrase "triadic structure" comes from H. Richard Niebuhr, *The Responsible Self: An Essay in Christian Moral Philosophy* (New York: Harper & Row, 1963). For the notion of the church as a community of moral discourse and discernment, see James M. Gustafson, *The Church as Moral Decision-Maker* (Philadelphia: Pilgrim Press, 1970) and below, chapter 7.

Discussion Questions for Chapter 1

1. Reflect a little on your own encounters with the catechism. What impressions of the catechism have remained with you through the years? To what extent, for example, would you categorize it as "individualistic and otherworldly"? Do you tend to think of it as relevant to modern social issues or more as a doctrinal standard of the church? As an interesting sixteenth-century testimony to the Reformed tradition but irrelevant, for the most part, to the social problems of the twentieth century? Explain your views.

2. Read James 2:14–26. Now read Romans 3:27–4:5. Note the similarities and the differences: Do James and Paul agree or disagree about the relation of faith and works? Do you think Paul and James mean the same thing by "faith"? Someone has suggested that to Paul faith without works is incomprehensible (see, for example, Gal. 5:6) and that to James faith without works is reprehensible. Do you agree? Do you think Paul and James are addressing different problems in the churches' common life? What problem is each addressing? Do those problems still exist in the church today? Which is more prominent in your church: the problem James addresses or the problem Paul addresses?

3. What does "the triadic structure" of the Christian life mean? Does our faith ever relate us only to God and not to our neighbors? Think about some of the ways we are related to God and about what that means for our relations to our neighbors. For example, I am related to God as creature to Creator; therefore, I am related to my neighbors as fellow creatures, creatures made by God and therefore to be highly regarded.

4. If you are a parent, what are some of the ways you've tried to teach your children the connection between faith and works, words and actions, doctrine and life?

2

COSTLY COMFORT

Q. *What is your only comfort*
in life and in death?

A. *That I am not my own,*
   but belong—
      body and soul,
      in life and in death—
to my faithful Savior Jesus Christ.

   He has fully paid for all my sins with his precious blood,
   and has set me free from the tyranny of the devil.
   He also watches over me in such a way
   that not a hair can fall from my head
   without the will of my Father in heaven:
   in fact, all things must work together for my salvation.

   Because I belong to him,
   Christ, by his Holy Spirit,
   assures me of eternal life
   and makes me whole-heartedly willing and ready
   from now on to live for him.
                           —Heidelberg Catechism Q & A 1

You are not your own; you were bought with a price. So glorify God in your
body.   *—1 Corinthians 6:19b–20*

11

We are not our own: let not our reason nor our will, therefore, sway our plans and deeds. We are not our own: let us therefore not set it as our goal to seek what is expedient for us according to the flesh. We are not our own: in so far as we can, let us therefore forget ourselves and all that is ours. Conversely, we are God's: let us therefore live for him and die for him. We are God's: let his wisdom and will therefore rule all our actions. We are God's: let all the parts of our life accordingly strive toward him as our only lawful goal.
—Calvin, Institutes, 3, vii, 1

To stress the bond between true doctrine and true practice is in no way a threat to the comfort of grace, but it is indeed a warning against taking comfort in cheap grace. —G.C. Berkouwer, "Orthodoxy and Orthopraxis"

THE OPENING QUESTION AND ANSWER of the Heidelberg Catechism seems an unlikely place to begin investigating our social responsibilities. Isn't this talk about "comfort" remote from the exacting challenges of economic justice, racial equality, or any quest for social righteousness? Who really thinks they will find "comfort" in addressing contemporary social problems?

As implausible as it sounds, however, when we take a more careful look at the catechism, we may discover that the comfort it talks about and offers is precisely the place for a Christian social ethic to begin.

Costly Comfort

When I think of "comfort," I think of my favorite chair; the warmth the wood-burner throws on a cold, wintry day; taking off my tie and shoes after working. But the catechism isn't referring to such "comforts." It's not talking about the comfort of "the comfortable pew" or the comfort the suburban church referred to in its advertisement:

Church of Christ
Air-conditioned
Worship in Comfort.

The comfort of the catechism does not promise us an easy life or a comfortable one; it promises to make us "willing and ready" to live for Christ.

We should be aware also of another misunderstanding of comfort. Because the catechism clearly teaches that comfort is free, that it is "a gift of grace" (Q & A 63), we are sometimes tempted to think of it as cheap. We are tempted to think that because this comfort is "by grace alone," we have nothing to do. After all, doesn't seeking merit in good works actually

12

threaten the Christian's comfort, putting him in the same camp as the social gospel liberals who think we can save and renew the world by our works? Indeed, sometimes we are tempted to think that, because the comfort is "by grace alone," we may do anything we like. Such an understanding of comfort is neatly captured in the crook's argument in W. H. Auden's poem, *For the Time Being*:

> I like committing crimes.
> God likes forgiving them.
> Really the world is admirably arranged.

The catechism, however, immediately undercuts any of our attempts to make its comfort either "comfortable" or "cheap." The comfort of which the catechism speaks is free, to be sure, but it is not cheap. It costs us our lives (we are not our own), as it cost Jesus his (for "he has fully paid for all my sins with his precious blood"). It leaves us free—not to do nothing and not to do anything we please, but to "live for him."

The comfort of which the catechism speaks is the costly (and offensive) comfort that we are not our own but belong to another. This costly comfort is nothing less than the kingly rule of Christ. The catechism itself makes that clear when it asks, "Why do you call him 'Our Lord'?" (Q 34). The answer echoes the comfort of the first reply: "Because . . . he has set us free from sin and from the tyranny of the devil, and has bought us, body and soul, to be his very own." The comfort of the catechism is the lordship of Jesus Christ—and that is the place for a Christian social ethic to begin.

No fear of moralism relieves us of our responsibility within the kingly rule of Christ to care for real people in their real needs. No suspicion of social gospel optimism delivers us from our obligation under his lordship to deliver power to the powerless or to stand with the poor and oppressed. Under the kingly rule of Christ—the comfort of the catechism—injustice has no place. This comfort demands that we face and meet the exacting and discomforting challenges of social righteousness. It's costly comfort, but it's real.

We'll find no real comfort in "cheap comfort." We'll find no real comfort in doing nothing or in doing what suits us and our interests—not even when the ostensible justification is "grace alone." The comfort of the catechism becomes ours not by speaking about it but by living in it. We will find comfort only in living and working and playing and dying as people who acknowledge and serve the kingly rule of Christ.

Self-Denial and Stewardship

The costly comfort of the catechism is that we are not our own. In other words, the *comfort* in the Christian life consists of *self-denial*.

Self-denial does not mean negating ourselves or despising ourselves, but rather forgetting ourselves and turning to God and our neighbors. Self-denial is not self-hatred. We would find no comfort in that. It is, rather, the self-forgetfulness of service to God and others. We can indeed find comfort in service—but no cheap comfort.

Calvin defines self-denial in terms of humility and love toward God and neighbor. "We are the stewards of everything God has conferred on us by which we are able to help our neighbor, and are required to render account of our stewardship" (3, vii, 5). Self-denial is stewardship, a stewardship that forgets self in helping others. We are not our own. Our power and prestige and prosperity are not our own. We are stewards, and our comfort requires and enables us to use those trusts for our neighbor's good.

Self-denial also and chiefly looks to God. It seeks not its own will but God's. And, according to Calvin, this "forms us to fairmindedness and tolerance" (III, vii, 8). For when we seek God's glory, how can we use the neighbor for our glory? Such self-denial uproots pride and sloth. It leaves no place for arrogance or ostentation. It provides the soil for humility and love, for nurturing the stewardship that regards the neighbor's well-being.

Then how may we rightly let our wishes and ambitions for our own "comfort" determine our social, political, economic, and racial decisions? Within the costly comfort of the catechism we may not. Calvin made the point most clearly: "We are not our own: let us therefore not set it as our goal to seek what is expedient for us according to the flesh" (3, vii, 1). Often our decisions about social policy are made simply and singly on the basis of our own interest. But the Christian comfort stands against such a simple, single criterion. We are not our own: something more and other than our prudent self-interest has to motivate and shape our social decisions and actions. That "something more and other" is the self-denial of stewardship.

Thus the gospel and the catechism turn the world's comfort upside down. The comfort of the catechism can only make the comfortable-according-to-the-flesh uneasy. It stands as challenge as well as promise to the holders of power and wealth and to the dealers in prestige and protocol. The comfort of the catechism judges the comfort of the proud and the comfort of the slothful and makes them—that is, us—"stewards of everything God has conferred on us by which we are able to help our neighbor."

The catechism, of course, is using a biblical phrase. "You are not your own" is Paul's line in 1 Corinthians 6:19. The text and its context do not allow any interpretation of the gospel or the catechism that would cheapen grace. On the contrary, it was precisely the "cheap comfort" of the Corinthian Christians that Paul was repudiating. The comfort of the gospel does not leave the Corinthians—or us—free to do whatever we like; it does not fit with unrighteousness; it does not fit with sloth or pride. The comfort of the gospel, "You are not your own," fits with the exacting demand to "shun immorality" (6:18).

This comfort presses hard upon us the obligations of everyday life. It makes us stewards of all God's gifts (specifically, in 1 Cor. 6, our sexuality).

14

We may not use our neighbor for our self-gratification. We must use God's gifts for the good of our neighbor and the glory of God. "You are not your own; you were bought with a price. So glorify God in your body."

Radical Monotheism

The catechism's costly comfort has another side. Not only are we "not our own," but we also belong to our faithful Savior Jesus Christ. That is our comfort. That is our confession. And it must be our real, working faith.

A person's real faith—whatever his "official faith"—is constituted by his loyalty to what he believes supremely valuable. A person's real morality—whatever her "official code"—is constituted by the ends and means with which she acts in loyalty to what she believes supremely valuable. In that sense, morality is always a function of faith.

The confession that we belong to our faithful Savior Jesus Christ ought to be our "real faith" and not just our "official faith." Sadly, we—no less than the people of God in Elijah's day—are tempted to divided loyalties. It seldom occurs to us that idolatry is as threatening a temptation today as in the time of Baal and Moloch. But in fact false gods are more menacing when using the fine arts of concealment and deception. We may not recite this first answer cavalierly. We must check for any subtle division that might run through our own hearts and lives.

We seldom examine with any care the other creeds and comforts that seduce us. We seldom make explicit or candid our "working faith" or our "real morality." If we were to make, for example, the "American Way of Life" our candid confession, it might look something like this:

My only comfort is my economic security and standard of living, which I achieve by hard work, friendliness, sharp business dealing, letting the buyer beware. It fully pays for all my gadgets—or almost all, anyway. I believe it is better to be young than old, rich than poor, white than black, American than anything else. I believe it is best to be comfortable. Oh yes, I believe in God, the kind, modern father who helps those who help themselves and blesses diligence and America; and in Jesus, who promises to take care of my soul when I die.

That creed is ripe for doubt—and yet it tempts and seduces us daily. It seems neatly to include "Christianity" without making us uncomfortable.

But Christianity and the catechism leave no room for such creeds. They make total claims. They insist that our only real comfort comes from belonging totally to the one true God. That is the radical monotheism of the Christian faith and the Heidelberg Catechism. And that radical monotheism demands that at the root of all our being and evaluating we worship the God who has shown himself to us in one faithful Savior, Jesus Christ.

Such radical monotheism has always been more of a hope than a reality among the people of God, more a possibility than an actuality. Again and again the people of God are faced with the lack of integrity between their "official faith" and their "working faith." Again and again the words of Elijah on Mt. Carmel stunningly clarify the issue: "How long will you go limping with two different opinions? If the LORD is God, follow him; but if Baal [or 'success' or 'money' or 'pleasure' or 'power'], then follow him" (1 Kings 18:21). Which will we choose? Whom or what will we serve in business and industry, in politics and development?

We usually try to avoid such a choice, to escape the costliness of the catechism's comfort, to cope with the uncomfortable tension between our official faith and real faith by making a handy compromise. The name of the compromise is "compartmentalization." One compartment is Sunday; the other is Monday through Saturday. On Sunday we acknowledge that the God of Abraham, Isaac, and Jacob raised Jesus from death; and in loyalty to him we zealously and sincerely pledge ourselves to love and justice. But on Monday morning we wake up in a different world, a world of business and busing, politics and pressure.

That moral problem has often been diagnosed as hypocrisy, as a gap between creed and deed. But the problem is more discerningly described as double-mindedness (cf. James 1:8) or as polytheism. The problem is not simply one of failing to live up to a creed; it is rather the problem of different creeds, different moralities—one for Sunday, one for the remainder of the week, and each acceptable on its home turf. The lack of integrity is not simply the inconsistency between creed and deed, but the inconsistency between creeds. The end is moral schizophrenia, the anarchy and duplicity of living by two creeds.

Somewhat subtler is the compartmentalization of life into private and public spheres. The Sunday creed has some effect Monday through Saturday in cultivating personal abstinence from certain specifiable "private" sins. But the Monday-to-Saturday creed takes over in the public domain. This dichotomy between private and public shrivels the Christian faith to an egotistical assurance that we are "saved." And gradually the Christian ethic dwindles to the pompous legalism that identifies the Christian life with the sepulchres whitewashed by abstinence from swearing, dirty jokes, sabbath-breaking, dancing.

Such compartmentalization allows the church to demand good private morality among its members, but it disentitles the church from dealing with public issues of economic, political, racial policy. It is a handy and altogether too popular device to resolve the conflict of loyalties. But it is no cure for moral schizophrenia.

However we attempt to avoid the shock that God raised Jesus in this world and in this history (and not even on the holy day, the Sabbath, but on the first day, Sunday), however we attempt to minimize the total claims of radical monotheism, it remains true, as we confess, that our only comfort is that we belong totally—body as well as soul, in life as well as in

16

death, weekday as well as Sunday, publicly as well as privately—to our faithful Savior Jesus Christ. We are not our own in the struggle between rich and poor; we are God's. We are not our own in the tension between powerful and powerless; we are God's. Compartmentalization is unacceptable to the catechism and to those who own the catechism as their confession. Decisions for Christ (or against him) take place in the cloakrooms and voting chambers of legislative assemblies as well as within consistory rooms.

All we do—all our evaluations and decisions and actions—must honor the one God who is gracious and sovereign (note the middle section of the catechism's reply to Q1). Because of his goodness and power, we dare to be servants in the world. Our comfort is our courage. We are not our own; we are God's. And God can be trusted. Therefore we set our minds, our devotion, our lives in the service of his glory and cause. We discipline our actions to enhance his power and kingdom. We are made "wholeheartedly willing and ready from now on to live for him."

The biblical passages echoed by the catechism again point the way to the social implications of the Christian faith. We misread Romans 14:7–9 if we take it individualistically, introspectively, "existentially." The passage stands in the context of Paul's admonitions to Jewish Christians and Gentile Christians, the "weak" and the "strong," neither to judge one another nor to despise one another. As there is one God and one crucified and risen Lord, so there is one community—a community marked by freedom, equality, and love. It is impossible to think that these Jews and Gentiles were "comfortable" with Paul's call to be an integrated community; but Paul demanded that they acknowledge that their only real comfort is their faithful Savior Jesus Christ.

First Corinthians 3:23 makes a similar point. In the context of the enmity between parties within the church, Paul reminds the Corinthian Christians that they are Christ's and Christ is God's. And the pattern of Christ the Lord is service, not pride. If we are Christ's, we may not boast, but we may dare to serve. Such at least is Paul's model and his unique defense of his apostleship in 1 Corinthians 1–4. We are exalted; indeed, all things are ours (1 Cor. 3:21,22). But we are Christ's. That is our comfort— and that comfort demands that we finally put everything under his lordship. We are exalted to servanthood.

Titus 2:11–19 links the Christian comfort, the grace of God which "has appeared for the salvation of all men," to the creation of "a people of his own who are zealous for good works." The comfort of the gospel is our courage to live lives that are in keeping with Christ's victory and lordship.

Costly Comfort and Investment

Here I ask you to consider your investment policy in the light of your costly comfort. It is important to point out that investments are only illustrative of the social implications of the catechism. We are not our own anywhere—in the voting booth, in corporate offices, in factories, in homes, on farms, in consistory rooms. We are Christ's everywhere. And we need to think, pray, and talk more seriously about what living this first Lord's Day means anywhere and everywhere.

Many Christian people and churches and institutions make investment decisions on the basis of two criteria only: security and yield. Some Christians have even tried to theologically justify such an investment policy. Many of them have modeled their arguments after John Wesley's "three plain rules": gain all you can, save all you can, give all you can! In other words, the higher the yield, the more with which to serve Christ's kingdom. But is such an investment policy acceptable to those who own the costly comfort of the catechism as their comfort?

Security and yield are sensible criteria, prudent criteria. But we are not our own. Our decisions, including our decisions about investments— about lending and borrowing, buying and selling—may not be made as though we were. The comfort of the catechism makes us stewards of our investments too. And being stewards means more than getting top dollar, and more even than giving a tithe. It means using our investments—and not just the profit from them—"to help our neighbor," to defend the powerless, to share with the poor.

Security and yield are sensible criteria, prudent criteria, but to those who would live the catechism, they are not sufficient criteria. The test for a "responsible investment" is not simply whether it's sufficiently secure or profitable but whether it is consistent with God's cause and glory, consistent with the criteria of love and justice. A "responsible investment" is one we make in response to the kingly rule of Christ, acknowledging that our comfort is that we are not our own but belong—also in saving and borrowing—to our faithful Savior.

Such a policy of "responsible investment" might lead us, for example, to make higher-risk, lower-yield investments in minority businesses, housing projects, conservation programs. It might lead us to refuse secure and profitable investments in corporations that enrich themselves at the expense of the third-world poor. It might lead us to attend that stockholders' meeting to protest a company policy that seriously damages the environment for the sake of higher profits. It might lead us to refuse that cheaper mortgage from a bank that refuses business loans to minorities. Or it might lead us to discipline the "slum-landlord" and support the landlord whose costly comfort, whose stewardship for the good of the neighbor, has made him vulnerable to financial loss.

The costly comfort of the catechism may lead us to some costly decisions in investments—and in other areas as well. What exactly those decisions are to be is not mine to say. But we must continue to recognize that it is not enough to memorize these words. We must take them to heart and try to live them. We are not our own. Neither are our investments.

Are we, as a church, ready to respond to the kingly reign of Christ, even in our buying and selling, borrowing and lending? Do we have the courage of our comfort?

Acknowledgments and Suggestions for Further Reading

The G. C. Berkouwer quote is from "Orthodoxy and Orthopraxis" in *God and the Good: Essays in Honor of Henry Stob*, edited by C. Orlebeke and L. Smedes (Grand Rapids: Wm. B. Eerdmans, 1975). The Auden Quote is from *The Collected Poetry of W. H. Auden* (New York: Random House, 1945), p. 459. The notion of "costly comfort" is dependent on Dietrich Bonhoeffer's treatment of "costly grace." See his *Cost of Discipleship* (New York: Macmillan, Inc., 1959), pp. 35–47. On the concept "radical monotheism" see the important and thoughtful—but somewhat difficult—book by H. Richard Niebuhr, *Radical Monotheism and Western Culture* (New York: Harper & Row, 1960).

The creed of the "American Way of Life" is indebted to Waldo Beach, *The Christian Life* (Richmond: The Covenant Life Curriculum Press, 1966), p. 12. This is a very readable and helpful book.

The John Wesley quote comes from his sermon "The Use of Money" in *Wesley's Standard Sermons*, edited by E. H. Sugden (London: Epworth Press, 1921), pp. 309–327. The mention of the use of Wesley's words to provide theological justification for an investment policy of security and yield makes it important to point out that the Pax World Fund of the United Methodist Church is a contemporary attempt to make ecclesiastical investments more responsive to other criteria.

On investment policy in general I recommend Charles Powers, *Social Responsibility and Investments* (Nashville: Abingdon Press, 1971). This book is a good tool for thinking about investment from a Christian perspective.

Discussion Questions for Chapter 2

1. What do you think about when you think of "comfort"? Is that close to or far from what you think the catechism means by "comfort"?

   "Comfort" is made up from two Latin words, *cum* and *fortis*. *Cum* means "with" and *fortis* means "strength." That would suggest that our comfort is that which strengthens us. Is that close to what the catechism means by "comfort"? Is our "comfort" our courage? What makes the comfort the catechism speaks of and offers "costly"?

2. What does "self-denial" mean and how is it relevant to our social responsibilities? How does self-denial, as Calvin says, form us into

stewards? What does "stewardship" mean? Is tithing stewardship? Can tithing become a kind of "compartmentalization"?

3. Discuss the creed of "The American Way of Life." How does it differ from the catechism? Would you call it a Christian creed? Do you agree that this creed "seduces us almost daily?" Explain.

Try writing a creed for some of the other "faiths" which tempt us, maybe one in which "happiness" or "pleasure" is supremely valuable.

4. Jesus said, "Do not lay up for yourselves treasure on earth, where moth and rust consume" (Matt. 6:19–21). He also told the parable of the talents, in which the master praises the servant who invested his talents wisely (Matt. 25:14–30). What investment policy can honor both passages as God's Word? Specifically, how should we earn, spend, borrow, and lend?

5. First Church is located in a changing neighborhood in a building that needs some significant repairs. Many of its members live south of the city. The church is trying to decide whether to sell its property and rebuild further south or to repair its sanctuary. If it repairs its present sanctuary, it must decide whether to do extensive (and expensive) remodeling to make the church utilizable as a day-care center, community center, etc. The investment is a substantial one for the church.

While investigating financing options, it discovers, almost accidentally, that one bank has a much better record of lending to minority businesses in its area than the other. But that bank would charge a slightly higher interest rate.

Should the church rebuild (move) or repair its existing facility? And if it decides to repair, which bank should it borrow from? Why? What other information do you wish you had to make this decision? Why would that information be relevant?

6. Many Christians have found genuine comfort in memorizing Q & A 1. You may want to do the same. It is a beautiful confession to know and to live by.

7. Try summarizing in your own words what you believe Q & A 1 has to say about our social responsibilities.

3

LOVE AND REALISM

Q. What does God's Law require of us?

A. Christ teaches us this in summary in Matthew 22—

> *You shall love the Lord your God*
> *with all your heart,*
> *and with all your soul,*
> *and with all your mind,*
> *and with all your strength.*
> *This is the great and first commandment.*
>
> *And a second is like it,*
> *You shall love your neighbor*
> *as yourself.*
>
> *On these two commandments depend*
> *all the law and the prophets.*
>
> *—Heidelberg Catechism Q & A 4*

Q. Can you live up to all this perfectly?
A. No.
> *I have a natural tendency*
> *to hate God and my neighbor.*
>
> *—Heidelberg Catechism Q & A 5*

Let every person be subject to the governing authorities. . . . Owe no one anything, except to love one another. . . . The night is far gone, the day is at hand.
—Romans 13:1a, 8a, 12a

Christian neighbor love demands that society do justice to its members. . . . Love demands that we be at pains to establish, or assist in establishing, a just social order. . . . The possession of a loving disposition toward the neighbor in one-to-one personal relations and the performance of personal acts of charity . . . never atones for the toleration of social injustices. *—Henry Stob, "The Dialectic of Love and Justice," p. 137*

Christianity is a religion which measures the total dimension of human existence not only in terms of the final norm of human conduct which is expressed in the law of love, but also in terms of the fact of sin.
—Reinhold Niebuhr, Why the Christian Church is Not Pacifist

THE SECOND LORD'S DAY of the Heidelberg Catechism sets side by side human sin and the law of love. God requires us to love, but we "have a natural tendency to hate." The catechism disowns the pride that would ignore or deny the fact of sin and the sloth that would excuse us from the law of love. Its combination of love and realism provides a vocation to justice.

To live the catechism, acknowledging the law of love and the fact of sin, will mean that we seek justice. That is the thesis of this chapter. I will develop it by looking briefly at one important American Christian ethicist, Reinhold Niebuhr; at the Calvinist political tradition; and at Romans 13:1–7. After examining those sources we will be ready to look more concretely at the social implications of this part of the catechism.

Reinhold Niebuhr on Love and Realism

Reinhold Niebuhr was one of America's greatest Christian ethicists. He broke with the American liberalism in which he was trained because he believed it was not sufficiently attentive to the reality and intransigence of human sin. His contribution to Christian social ethics in this country can be construed as an extended commentary on Lord's Day 2, for he consistently held that the law of love was the final norm of human conduct and that human beings and communities are sinful and prone to selfishness and pride. Some of the social implications of that combination of love and realism become obvious in Niebuhr's argument against pacifism.

Niebuhr begins his little book *Why the Christian Church is Not Pacifist* by agreeing both with the catechism and with the pacifist views of American liberals: he acknowledges that the law of love is an absolute and uncompromising moral standard. Jesus has taught us that God requires people to love God and their neighbor.

We may not, Niebuhr continues, water down the stringency of this requirement: Jesus demands agape—the self-giving, non-calculating love that mirrors God's love for sinners. He demands that we love our enemies, that we forgive seventy times seven, that we bless those who curse us and do good to those who hate us. He demands absolutely perfect love.

So far the pacifists, the catechism, and Reinhold Niebuhr all walk the same path.

But then Niebuhr takes a decisive further step with the catechism, leaving pacifism behind. Such love is "impossible," he says. People are sinners and prone to pride, prone to self-centeredness, prone to hate God and neighbor. The law of love remains our obligation, but it is not a simple historical possibility. None of us lives up to that law perfectly. No human action—no matter how much better than alternative actions at the time—is completely free of pride and selfishness. All social groups—the family, the tribe, the clan, the ethnic group, the race, the nation—tend to be proud and selfish; in fact, social groups are even less able to restrain their self-interest than individuals are. So the love that Jesus commanded is not possible in such a world, either personally or politically.

Niebuhr's main criticism of pacifism, then, is that it lacks realism, that it ignores the reality of sin in considering perfect love a simple political option. The pacifist refusal to use coercion against a tyrant in this world underestimates the reality and power of sin. Unwittingly, it lets tyranny win and, in effect, surrenders the world to sin. The refusal to use power in this kind of world is a refusal to accept responsibility for restraining the greed and pride of some in order to protect our neighbor. Such a refusal means complicity in this world's evils.

Love is impossible, but it is not for that reason irrelevant, according to Niebuhr. Love remains relevant and normative both as an "indiscriminate principle of criticism" and as a "principle of discriminate criticism."

As an "indiscriminate principle of criticism," the law of love presents the ultimate standard by which all our actions and social policies are judged—and found wanting. The law reveals to us our selfishness. It shows us our "misery" (as the catechism would say), our "tragic situation" (as Niebuhr more frequently says).

This indiscriminate criticism performs a great service for morality and for the gospel. First, it keeps us from self-righteousness and complacency; love reminds us that we may never be satisfied with any personal or social status quo. And, second, it prepares us for the gospel—which is not the law of love itself, but the news that God's grace justifies people who are unable to love rightly.

Love, then, reveals that no social policy is perfect. But as a "principle of discriminate criticism," love also reveals that some actions and policies are better than others. In a sinful world where perfect love is not a simple political option, the closest possible approximation is a society of equal justice. Such a society will not be without egoism and coercion. It will still fall under the indiscriminate criticism of self-giving love. But its equal and fair limitations on each one for the protection of each other one is an expression of love, indeed a demand of love, in a world that is prone to hate.

Because Niebuhr believes both that love is normative and that love is not a simple possibility for sinful people, he recognizes the obligation to seek justice, to work for those fair restraints on egoism that are possible in a sinful world. Such justice, of course, requires the use of coercion and sometimes even war. That's why Niebuhr is not a pacifist and, so he argues, why the church should not be pacifist.

The Calvinist Political Tradition

Those who confess Lord's Day 2 are driven to make similar observations and to hear the same vocation to justice. God's law is love. It does not cease being God's law because we are unable to live up to it. The catechism's realism about human sin does not excuse us from the obligation to love our neighbor. The catechism does not water down the stringency of God's law in the interest of some cheap comfort. It requires nothing less than love.

But the catechism is also realistic about human sin. It will not allow us to think we or our societies have achieved God's will for our lives. It requires nothing less than repentance.

The catechism's intention here, of course, is to show us our sin and misery so that we may hear the gospel of deliverance, the good news that the triumph of love was and is a *divine* possibility (see Qs & As 11, 15, 17). But this conjunction of the law of love and realism about human sin also destroys complacency or arrogance about the social status quo. Perhaps we don't intend that to happen. Perhaps we only intend to hear about deliverance. But there is no way, according to the catechism, to hear the gospel without first hearing the very thing that destroys our comfortable self-righteousness.

For a social ethic faithful to the catechism, the law of love remains the standard by which to test our social actions, policies, and states of affairs. By that standard, and in the judgment of the catechism, all our social actions, policies, and states of affairs are found wanting. This judgment destroys our complacency with the status quo, frees us, and calls us to work for a relatively more loving society—a society with better protections for the poor and powerless, a society with more equitable distribution of political and economic power, a society, in short, of equal justice.

Such a society will not be without selfishness; it will not be without coercion; it will still fall short of perfect love. But its equal and fair limitations on each one for the protection of each other one will be an expression of love in a world where people are prone to hate. The catechism's acknowledgment of the law of love and its realism about human sin combine, then, to call God's people to justice.

That same combination of love and realism prompted early Calvinistic political theory and political action. It was Calvin's realism about kings and their egotistic and selfish use of power that led him to prefer a system compounded of aristocracy and democracy. "Men's fault or failing causes it to be safer and more bearable for a number to exercise government" (4, xx, 8).

Later Calvinists developed that insight into doctrines of checks and balances and constitutional democracy. They viewed the power of government as a relative good for the protection of each neighbor in a world of selfishness, as a tool of love that promotes and protects the equity of each neighbor.

That attitude toward government frequently led Calvin's followers to criticize particular governments and particular legislation and, in fact, sometimes to rebel, initiating a tradition of dynamic relation between religion and politics. This tradition was carried on by men like Beza, "Junius Brutus," Knox, Rutherford, and early Dutch and American Calvinists. Reinhold Niebuhr once said of these men and their tradition:

Perhaps the most impressive social ethic of the Reformation was that which developed in seventeenth-century Calvinism. This form of Calvinism revealed itself in the struggles with Catholic princes in Scotland, in Holland, and in the Cromwellian revolution in England. It laid the foundation for a free society and for toleration in the religious sphere, without which a modern pluralistic national community would not be possible. . . . It is the only form of Protestant social ethic which I find congenial to present perplexities.

The love and realism of the catechism oblige us to build on that foundation. Of course, we now have constitutional democracies, but that doesn't mean we have no more to do. The radical demands of neighbor love ought to keep us from both sloth and pride, making us sensitive to unequal distribution of political and economic power. The persons and churches who confess Lord's Day 2 in a world like this one commit themselves to the quest for justice.

Romans 13 and Lord's Day 2

Sometimes that tradition of a dynamic relationship between religion and politics has been hidden and forgotten behind a misunderstanding of Romans 13:1–7. People have insisted that Romans 13 calls for uncritical devotion to government, for political quietism, or even for un- qualified endorsement of an evil regime. But Romans 13 needs to be read within the context of the duty to love and realism about human sin. It needs to be read within the context of Lord's Day 2.

Of course, it needs also to be read within the context of the whole canon, and it is there that we should begin. Other biblical passages may help prevent us from reading Romans 13:1–7 as a warrant for an unquali- fied endorsement of whatever rulers happen to hold power. The prophets, for example, repeatedly say that rulers are subject to God and particularly subject to his wrath and judgment when they oppress the poor and the powerless. And Revelation 13 depicts the Roman government as the beast. When passages of Scripture critical of particular rulers are set alongside Romans 13:1–7, the church may recognize the moral ambiguity of political power and our responsibility to be discerning as we respond to particular "powers that be."

It is important, of course, to see the moral ambiguity of govern- ments. And it is noteworthy that in the biblical account of the institution of the monarchy (1 Sam. 8–10), that ambiguity is pronounced. On the one hand, the people's demand for a king was an affront to God, the one king of Israel. On the other hand, it was God's will that Saul became king.

To see the ambiguity of government, however, can confuse us. It can make us feel as though we are simply limping between attitudes of unquestioning submission and rebellious resentment. What we need is some direction in the midst of ambiguity, some standard to guide discern- ment. The story of the anointing of Saul contains such a lesson. Saul, after all, was the son of "the humblest of all the families" of "the least of the tribes" (1 Sam. 9:21). The lesson of this, the direction, the standard, is that God exalts the poor and humbles the exalted. That lesson is quite different from the world's conventional perspective on rank and power. Within the world's perspective the question some of the Israelites asked, "How can this man save us?" (10:27), was quite understandable. But under God's plan and provision, power exists for service, for raising the poor and defending the powerless, for the cause of neighbor love in a world threatened by sin. That biblical perspective on power can give direction and judgment to political discernment.

Romans 13 teaches the same lesson, provides the same direction for political discernment, when it is read in the context of Lord's Day 2. Such a context—the demand to love and the realism about human sin—is not alien. Paul himself brackets the passage with commands to love our neighbor (12:9, 13:8) and concludes with the eschatological prohibition of pride and sloth (13:11–14).

Many have observed that the ideas about government found in Romans 13:1–7 are similar to those found in the conventional wisdom of Hellenistic Judaism. Both sources teach that governments have their au- thority from God, that they exist to encourage the good and punish the evil, and that those who benefit from the order and security the government provides should be willing to pay taxes and render due honor and respect. Paul, then, would seem simply to be instructing the Roman churches to stick to the tradition that formed their political posture.

But Paul puts that tradition, that conventional wisdom, into a new context, a transforming context. He sets before and behind their tradition the duty to love and reminds them of the approach of the end. Every encounter with our neighbor, Paul implies, should occur in the expectancy of Christ's coming. Until he comes, we must continue to love in a selfish world. Until he comes, we must struggle against principalities and powers and dominions.

So Paul puts submission to government into the context of love and the recognition of the "not-yet" character of our world. Our obligation to government stands in the context of our more basic obligation to love our neighbor while we await the consummation of God's great victory over sin. That is the only kind of obligation the gospel requires or condones. Government is to be a tool of love by protecting each neighbor in a world of selfishness and enmity. The law of God is neighbor-love. So, Paul teaches, seek the welfare of your neighbor in a world not yet free from sin. Be politically responsible for the good of your neighbor.

Paul has set the institutionally oriented advice of Hellenistic Judaism within the neighbor orientation and end-time orientation of the gospel. That's decisive for him—and for the Calvinist political tradition. We are to love our neighbor in a world not yet free from sin.

So we are given a vocation to justice.
So we are made politically responsible.
So we may live Lord's Day 2.

Concrete Love in a World of Selfishness

The catechism's acknowledgment of the law of love and its realism about human sin provide us with a vocation to justice. That's both the thesis of this chapter and an important social implication of the catechism. So far we've treated that implication in a general and abstract way. But we must do more. The catechism here has concrete implications in areas as different as family relations, race relations, and world hunger.

In the family, where the spirit of love is perhaps strongest, the careful calculation of rights and duties and the equitable apportioning of them is, nevertheless, an important matter—as anyone with three children and two candies will testify. Love in a world of selfishness demands justice. Every parent knows that. No structure of justice is perfect. Every child knows that. Imperfect structures of justice can be changed under the transforming criticism of love and can be made more tolerable by the spirit of love. Every healthy family knows that.

27

If justice is necessary in the family, think how much more it is required in race relations. We are to love the black child growing up in the city. That does not mean white members of the Christian Reformed Church may find cheap comfort or easy conscience in assuring themselves that they are not racist because they think "all little black children are adorable." We keep God's law by perfect love, and in a selfish world that means we are alert to the group interests and egotisms that have made a black child not just a resident but a captive of the city. Loving a black child in a world like this one means engaging in a political quest for justice, for the sort of society where that child can flourish and where, at the very least, his rights will be respected and his legitimate claims to fair and equal opportunities will be satisfied.

It is good (indeed, required) that the church is composed of different races and ethnic groups. It is good (indeed, required) that our one-to-one relations with members of another race can be relatively more loving in the church. It is good (indeed, required) that acts of charity can mark our life together. But the catechism still reminds us of our duty to love our neighbors—all of them, even the neighbors we don't know—and of our tendency, and the tendency of all people, to hate. The catechism reminds us of our duty to love the unknown neighbor who is still threatened by human greed or violence or apathy. The catechism reminds us, thus, of our vocation to justice. To live the catechism will mean that we work together in the church, black and white and Hispanic and Oriental, for justice in our world. We will live the catechism when we work together as God's people to secure for that child we never met an opportunity for an adequate education, for adequate housing, for adequate health care, and eventually for rewarding work. Loving our neighbor in a racist world means insisting that racial justice be done.

Fighting racism is not merely a nice thing to do if we have time and money; it is an expression of our confessional integrity. The same confessional integrity will keep us both from the pride of thinking that we have lived up to the law of God in race relations because we have a church committee devoted to that cause and from the sloth of thinking that, because we cannot love perfectly, God's law is not normative for us. It is not enough to memorize the words of the catechism. We must try to live them. And trying to live Lord's Day 2 will mean trying to love in a world of enmity.

Finally, consider our obligation to love the fifteen thousand people who will die today of hunger. Fifteen thousand died of hunger the day I said, "I can't eat another bite. I'm too full." Fifteen thousand will die today before I end the day with a bedtime snack and a prayer for the hungry. Suppose Jesus' parable had been about a rich man and fifteen thousand Lazaruses. The obligation to love each one would not have been relaxed, I'm sure. And the point of the parable, I'm afraid, would remain not so much the consolation of the poor as the judgment against the rich. The perfect love Jesus demands judged the rich man and judges me. Moses and the prophets demanded justice for the poor, but the rich man said,

" 'But if someone goes to them from the dead, they will repent' " (Luke 16:30). Now one has been raised from the dead—the very one who said God's law is love. Are we convinced?

Again certain signs and symptoms of confessional integrity should be applauded. Some churches have sponsored fasts as a gesture of their sympathy with the hungry and have sent the money saved to an organization equipped to fight world hunger. Many have joined Bread for the World as a way of influencing legislation and policy toward relieving world hunger. Church workers have been involved in relief and development, feeding the hungry and providing resources and training for them so they can begin to feed themselves. Such actions are good (and required); but again, Lord's Day 2 permits us neither the pride of thinking we have fulfilled our obligations nor the sloth of thinking that because love is not a simple historical possibility, God's law is not relevant to the problem of world hunger.

Perfect love stands in judgment on international policies that serve only the rich nations and multinational corporations. Love reproaches Christian approval of tariff and quota systems that effectively keep the poor nations poor. In a world like this one love requires us to work for universal and inclusive justice.

When Christ asks us, "Did you love the fifteen thousand Lazaruses? Did you feed them? Did you give them to drink?," it will not be acceptable to answer, "Well, we did give them just under two-tenths of one percent of our gross national product." The catechism's confession that love is normative and its realism about human sin give us a vocation to international economic justice. To say that such justice doesn't belong on the church's agenda is to ignore the realism of the catechism. It's not enough to memorize these words. We must try to live them.

Acknowledgments and Suggestions for Further Reading

The citation of Henry Stob is from "The Dialectic of Love and Justice" in his *Ethical Reflections* (Grand Rapids: Wm. B. Eerdmans, 1978), p. 137. That whole chapter along with earlier chapters on "The Concept of Love: Eros and Agape" and "The Concept of Justice" provide valuable insights into the meaning and relation of love and justice.

Reinhold Niebuhr has written a great deal. The little book referred to in the text, *Why the Christian Church is Not Pacifist* (London: Student Christian Movement Press, 1940), is quite readable. So is the more general *An Interpretation of Christian Ethics* (New York: Harper Brothers, 1935). His greatest work, however, something of an American theological classic, is *The Nature and Destiny of Man* (New York: Charles Scribner's Sons, 1941). The quote in which Niebuhr praises the Calvinist political tradition is taken from his "The Problem of a Protestant Social Ethic", *Union Seminary Quarterly Review*, XV (November, 1959), p. 5. One can get a good introduction to Niebuhr's thought—and see it applied to questions ranging from communism and the Hungarian revolt to race relations and fair employment practices to nuclear weapons and strategic pacifism—in two collections of his articles edited by D. B. Robertson, *Love and Justice* (New York: Meridian Books, 1967) and *Applied Christianity* (New York: Meridian Books, 1959).

It should be observed that Niebuhr was responding to the pacifism of American liberalism, not the pacifism of Mennonites like John Yoder. The reader may wish to consult the work of Yoder for a defense of pacifism which does not ignore or deny the intransigence of human sin. See Yoder, *The Christian Witness to the State* (Newton, Kansas: Faith and Life Press, 1964) and *The Politics of Jesus* (Grand Rapids: Wm. B. Eerdmans, 1972). Mennonite pacifism is not so much a political policy as a witness. It wants to be judged in terms of the authenticity of its witness rather than in terms of the success of pacifism as a policy in attaining good and avoiding evil consequences.

It may also be observed that in 1939, one year before the publication of Niebuhr's *Why the Christian Church is Not Pacifist*, the Christian Reformed Church adopted a position that distanced it from the pacifism of the time. Its argument included reference to the law of love and realism about human nature. It accused pacifists of being "inclined to forget that in the face of unjust aggression the law of love may actually urge a demand for forcible resistance" (*Acts of Synod 1939*). The excellent statement of 1982 similarly begins from the law of love and realism about human sin (*Acts of Synod 1982*, pp. 615–621).

On the Calvinist political tradition the primary sources include Book IV, Chapter 20 of *Calvin: Institutes of the Christian Religion*, edited by John T. McNeill, translated by Ford Lewis Battles (Philadelphia: The Westminster Press, 1960; *Library of Christian Classics*, Vols. XX and XXI); John Calvin, *Commentaries on the Book of the Prophet Daniel* (6:20,21), vol. 1 (Wm. B. Eerdmans, 1948); Christopher Goodman, *How Superior Powers Oght to be Obeyd* (New York: for Facsimile Text Society, Columbia University Press, 1931); Harold J. Laski, ed., "Junius Brutus," *A Defense of Liberty against Tyrants* (New York: Harcourt & Brace, 1925). Among secondary sources one might consult Winthrop S. Hudson, "Democratic Freedom and Religious Faith in the Reformed Tradition," *Church History*, XV (1946),177–194, and Herbert Darling Foster, "The Political Theories of Calvinists Before the Puritan Exodus to America," *American Historical Review*, Vol. XXI, No. 3 (April 1916), 481–503. On Romans 13 one might consult the work of Verhey cited earlier as well, of course, as Calvin's commmentary on the passage. Two other valuable treatments are Hans-Werner Bartsch, "A New Theological Approach to Christian Social Ethics" in John C. Bennett, ed., *Christian Social Ethics in a Changing World*

(London: SCM Press, 1966), pp. 59–77, and Victor Paul Furnish, *The Moral Teaching of Paul* (Nashville: Abingdon, 1979), pp. 115–141.

On the concrete questions dealt with, see "Declarations on Race," *Acts of Synod of the Christian Reformed Church 1968*, pp. 17ff; "Declaration on World Hunger," *Acts of Synod 1978*, pp.79–86; "For My Neighbor's Good," *Acts of Synod 1979*, pp.82–84, 610–641.

Discussion Questions for Chapter 3

1. Spend some time identifying the relatively powerless in your community. Who are they? Do they have anything like equal opportunities in education and jobs? Are they the last hired and the first laid off? Do they have access to adequate housing at reasonable rates?

   Review specific ways your congregation is reaching out to the poor and the powerless in your area. Should the church's love for such persons take the shape of charity or of insistence that at least justice be done for them? Finally, what suggestions do you have for improving the church's ministry—your ministry—to these community people?

2. The second Lord's Day of the catechism ought to have some bearing on our stance on war (especially nuclear war) and the arms race. Consider one or more of the following areas for discussion:

Pacifism

Christians who are not pacifists ordinarily use some form of "just war theory" to think about particular wars. Some of the criteria are: a. just cause (usually limited to defense against aggression) b. last resort c. proportionality (that is, the evil done by waging war must not outweigh the good sought by fighting it) and d. non-combatant immunity (that is, those not engaged in fighting the war may not be harmed or injured).

Niebuhr rejected pacifism in 1940. In light of the changing nature of war, should we reject it today?

Just vs. Unjust War

It is sometimes difficult to decide whether a particular war is just or unjust according to the criteria of a just war. If it is our duty to love in a world of enmity, should we presume

a.that we shouldn't fight in a war until we are firmly convinced that the war is just, or

b. that we should fight when our nation tells us to fight unless we are firmly convinced that the war is unjust?

Nuclear War

According to the criteria above (especially proportionality and non-combatant immunity), can a nuclear war ever be a just war? If not, should

31

we adopt a policy of "nuclear pacifism"? And, if we should take the position that the use of nuclear weapons cannot be morally justified, can the threat to use them be morally justified? May we support a national policy of building and deploying more nuclear weapons? May we support "the nuclear freeze"?

Some people refuse to pay part of their income tax proportionate to the share of the national budget spent on nuclear weapons; in the light of Romans 13:1–7 and its context, do you think that decision is justifiable?

Arms Race

What light does the catechism's realism throw on public debate about the arms race? On the one hand, is the suggestion of some that the US should unilaterally disarm realistic enough about human sin? Or, is such a suggestion overly optimistic and naive about the human and national will for power? On the other hand, is the view that we must develop new weapons in order to assure that we will never have to use them realistic enough about human capacities for evil? Or, is that view overly optimistic and naive about the capacities of politicians to resist forever using their most effective weapons when the chips are down? What is the realistic policy which would most closely approximate the demands of love?

3. Church relief committees or agencies typically develop programs in areas to enhance nutrition and health, to provide literacy, and to generate income. These are worthy programs. Sometimes the work is stymied by local injustice and lack of respect for human rights. Should a church agency make a prophetic witness against injustice in places where it conducts its mission? If so, what form would such a prophetic witness take? May we ever encourage civil disobedience? Should we ignore social injustice in order to preach the gospel to individuals or to provide relief for the victims of natural disasters or human injustice?

4. This chapter and the previous questions have suggested several areas related to Lord's Day 2 and social responsibility: race relations, poverty and hunger, war and peace. Take some time to reflect on these applications (or others) and to think about how they touch your life as a church member and as an individual. Perhaps there is one area related to Lord's Day 2 in which you could resolve to "live the catechism" with renewed commitment. Make a note to yourself of one positive thing you could *do* differently or more completely. If you wish, share your idea with others in your group. Then promise yourself to put your idea into action.

4

RESPONSIBILITY

Q. Did God create man
    so wicked and perverse?

A. No.
    God created man good and in his own image,
        that is, in true righteousness and holiness,
    so that he might
        truly know God his creator,
        love him with all his heart,
        and live with him in eternal happiness
    for his praise and glory.

    —Heidelberg Catechism Q & A 6

Q. Then where does man's corrupt nature
    come from?

A. From the fall and disobedience of our first parents,
        Adam and Eve, in Paradise.
    This fall has so poisoned our nature
        that we are born sinners—
        corrupt from conception on.

    —Heidelberg Catechism Q & A 7

Q. But are we so corrupt
   that we are totally unable to do any good
   and inclined toward all evil?

A. Yes, unless we are born again,
   by the Spirit of God.

—*Heidelberg Catechism Q & A 8*

Q. But doesn't God do man an injustice
   by requiring in his law
   what man is unable to do?

A. No, God created man with the ability to keep the law.
   Man, however, tempted by the devil,
      in reckless disobedience,
      robbed himself and his descendants of these gifts.

—*Heidelberg Catechism Q & A 9*

Q. Will God permit
   such disobedience and rebellion
   to go unpunished?

A. Certainly not.
   He is terribly angry
      about the sin we are born with
      as well as the sins we personally commit.

   As a just judge
   he punishes them now and in eternity.

   He has declared:
      "Cursed be every one who does not abide by
      all things written in the book of the law,
      and do them."

—*Heidelberg Catechism Q & A 10*

Q. According to God's righteous judgment
   we deserve punishment
   both in this world and forever after:
   how then can we escape this punishment
   and return to God's favor?

A. God requires that his justice be satisfied.
   Therefore the claims of his justice
   must be paid in full,
   either by ourselves or by another.

—*Heidelberg Catechism Q & A 12*

Q. Can we pay this debt ourselves?

A. Certainly not.
   Actually, we increase our guilt every day.
                          —*Heidelberg Catechism Q & A 13*

Q. And who is this mediator—
   true God and at the same time
   truly human and truly righteous?

A. Our Lord Jesus Christ,
   who was given us
   to set us completely free
   and to make us right with God.
                          —*Heidelberg Catechism Q & A 18*

Q. How do you come to know this?

A. The holy gospel tells me.
   God himself began to reveal the gospel already in Paradise;
   later, he proclaimed it
      by the holy patriarchs and prophets,
   and portrayed it
      by the sacrifices and other ceremonies of the law;
   finally, he fulfilled it
      through his own dear Son.
                          —*Heidelberg Catechism Q & A 19*

When I look at thy heavens, the work of thy fingers,
   the moon and the stars which thou hast established;
what is man that thou art mindful of him,
   and the son of man that thou dost care for him?

Yet thou hast made him little less than God,
   and dost crown him with glory and honor.
Thou hast given him dominion over the works of thy hands;
   thou hast put all things under his feet,
all sheep and oxen,
   and also the beasts of the field,
the birds of the air, and the fish of the sea,
   whatever passes along the paths of the sea.
                          —*Psalm 8:3–8*

The depravity and malice both of man and of the devil, or the sins that arise therefrom, do not spring from nature, but rather from the corruption of nature.

—*John Calvin*, Institutes, 1, xiv, 3

My neighbor is . . . the image of God on earth. . . . As a person my neighbor does not have to carry a report card to prove that he performs well, or an identity card to certify his bloodline, or papers to show he belongs to the church. No matter whether he is beautiful or ugly, wise or foolish, strong or weak. All he need be is a person born of a woman; if so, he has rights to be respected as an inviolable human self that is only a little lower than the angels (Ps. 8:5).

—*Lewis Smedes*, Mere Morality

NO ONE CAN DENY that it's a sad world. Wars and rumors of war, little children whose lives are crippled—or ended—by hunger or oppression, broken homes and broken dreams, the bitterness and injustice of racism, and countless other evils make our life together eloquent testimony to the fall.

And no one can deny our responsibility for it and in it—at least not if we are faithful to the catechism. Our response to God does not entitle us to disown responsibility in and for this world. It holds us to it. And "the Spirit of God" makes us able to respond to God in faith and to exercise that response-ability in and for God's world (Q & A 8).

"Misery" and Responsibility

Some people acknowledge the sadness of this world but refuse to acknowledge their complicity in it. They own the "misery" of the human condition, but try to disown any responsibility for it. In Lord's Days 3 and 4 the catechism responds with a categorical "no" to all who would insinuate, whether slothfully or rebelliously, that all this is God's fault. We may not indict God. "God created man good and in his own image." And God's intention in creation was that people might know him, love him, and live with him. That is God's praise and glory (Q & A 6). The one who cast this world into existence, the one who stands behind our lives and our life together, is himself good and worthy of our trust and praise.

Because God made people good and in his own image, we are responsible. But we made evil out of good. We sinned. And we are responsible for the corruption of our nature and of our life together. Adam's sin was a free act of disobedience by which we stood against God and his intentions for his creation. It was an act of "reckless disobedience" (Q & A 9). And by that free act evil entered the world and corrupted the good.

36

Evil is—and must be—parasitic on the good in a world created by God out of nothing. Parasites, of course, are dangerous and can destroy the good (and themselves as well when the good is no more). But sin is by no means the first word about us. God's love is. We remain God's creatures—responsible but corrupt!

Adam's sin sometimes seems a trifling matter, but through it the parasite infected the good nature God created (Q & A 7). And that parasite flourished and erupted in murder. If we were ever tempted to think individualistically, the catechism's sobering confession of our corruption through Adam's sin should rescue us. And if we were still tempted to think individualistically, Cain's response "Am I my brother's keeper?" should humble us. We are responsible. God created us with the ability to respond in love and faith to him and to exercise that response-ability in and for his world. Neither the corruption of Adam's first sin, nor the enmity of Cain's murder of Abel, nor the apathy of his response can change that fundamental fact about us. We are responsible.

We are responsible to God, and therefore we know something of what we are responsible for. God created humans good; our responsibility to God the creator makes us responsible for affirming and nurturing the dignity and unity of all the sons and daughters of Adam. Of course, humans have fallen; all are corrupted with Adam; each is incorrigibly depraved.

But recognizing our depravity does not remove our responsibility to God the creator. Indeed, recognizing our depravity helps us stand guard against all elitisms. It helps us refrain from exalting ourselves or despising our neighbor.

Of course, such self-love and neighbor-hate are exactly the parasite that infects us, and we continually give assent to Adam's corruption of our life together. Our allegiances to "our kind of people" or "the right kind of people" are corrupt when they allow slogans or support policies that preserve our privileges and prerogatives at the expense of others. If we are to respond faithfully to God the creator, then we are responsible for the unity and equality of all persons.

The catechism teaches that sin is not the first word, the originating word, about us. It also teaches that sin is not the last word about us. It knows that God cannot and will not tolerate sin. Far from us indicting God, the catechism announces God's indictment on us. The misery of our life together, the sadness of this world, is our own responsibility, and about sin God is "terribly angry" (Q & A 10).

The catechism is not apologetic about mentioning God's anger or wrath (cf. Qs & As 14, 17, 37). Sometimes Christians have been offended by this concept and have thought that anger is somehow unworthy of a loving God. But the catechism knows that God's mercy could not remain God's mercy if it compromised with unrighteousness. The catechism knows that if God is not to allow people and his intentions with people to be violated, then he may not allow his justice to be violated. So God the creator gets angry about human sin—and must if sin is not to have the last word. God the creator is also God the judge—and must be to preserve his creation, to restrain the effects of sin, and to fulfill his intentions.

If we are to respond to God the judge faithfully, then we are responsible for disclosing and fighting sin in all its forms. Indeed, in this sad world, responding to God, the creator and judge, means that we must get angry about racism, get indignant about injustice, and hate those social sins that infect our common life and harm our neighbors.

The catechism knows that God is a good creator and a righteous judge, and it knows that people are responsible to God the creator and judge. Nothing can remove or minimize this responsibility. We must love and respect God's creation, and we must hate the parasite that threatens it.

"Deliverance" and Responsibility

So far we have only hinted at the really remarkable thing. God is the creator and the judge, and we are responsible to him. But the remarkable thing is that God is our deliverer too. The remarkable thing is deliverance in "our Lord Jesus Christ" (Q & A 18). In him God's justice is also our deliverance and our righteousness.

The catechism makes it plain that God delivers us not *from* our responsibilities but *for* them. This deliverance in Jesus Christ sets us "completely free" (Q & A 18)—not free from our responsibilities but "free from the tyranny of the devil" (Q & A 1). It makes us "right with God" (Q & A 18) through genuine restoration to "righteousness and life" (Q & A 17). Christ and his Spirit (Q & A 8) renew us in our response-ability. The catechism knows that God is the creator and judge and deliverer, and it calls us to respond to him in faith and to exercise our response-ability in all areas of our lives.

Deliverance is the heart of the gospel and the heart of the cate-chism. True to the gospel, the catechism proclaims that deliverance is not (and cannot be) our achievement. It is a gift of "sheer grace" (Q & A 21); it is the justification of the unjust. God "justifies the ungodly" (Rom. 4:5). Calvin called such deliverance "the main hinge on which religion turns" (3, xi, 1); but neither Calvin nor the catechism nor the gospel makes any attempt to remove the shocking and scandalous character of such justifica-tion. Jesus said, "I came not to call the righteous, but sinners" (Mark 2:17). His hearers were doubtlessly shocked, and the announcement of such a gospel has been shocking ever since. It is shocking because the law is clear: judges are to acquit the innocent and condemn the guilty (Deut. 25:1). But God, the judge of all the earth, acquits the guilty. How can God act like that? How can he justify the unrighteous without wrecking the very stan-dards of justice that preserve his creation and restrain that parasite evil?

The catechism doesn't ignore that problem. It knows that "God requires that his justice be satisfied" (Q & A 12), and it echoes God's own words, "I will not acquit the wicked" (Ex. 23:7). Justification cannot come at the expense of either God's righteousness or human responsibility. It is in the Lord Jesus Christ, "truly human and truly righteous" and "true God" (Qs & As 15, 18), that God establishes both himself and his human creatures in the right. Those are the affirmations of the catechism: that God is just in Christ, and that we are justified and restored to righteousness and response-ability in Christ.

God could simply have said, "That's OK. Forget it"—but only by denying his own justice and by ceasing to treat us as responsible moral agents. Certainly he could justly have left us in our sin and death and hell, but from the very beginning he committed himself to a people who could know him, love him, and exercise response-ability to him for his whole creation (Q & A 6).

In Jesus, God does not demean us to save us; he does not remove our responsibility; rather he holds us to it and renews it. In Jesus, God judges us, to be sure; but in Jesus, the claims of his justice are paid. In Jesus, God himself bears the hurt, the shame, the curse; but he bears it humanly, as it must be borne (Q & A 16). And God himself wins the victory by his great power which raised Jesus from the dead. The crucified one has been raised. In him we are judged—and exalted, renewed, restored. "As by a man came death, by a man has come also the resurrection of the dead" (1 Cor. 15:21; referred to in Q & A 16). Christ "was put to death for our trespasses and raised for our justification" (Rom. 4:25). He "restores to us righteousness and life" (Q & A 17).

In Jesus, God establishes both his righteousness and ours. To be sure, the righteousness in Christ is "apart from law" (Rom. 3:21), but it does not overthrow either the law or human responsibility. On the contrary, the law and the prophets bear witness to such a righteousness (Rom. 3:21; Q & A 19). We are both upheld by and held to such a righteousness.

God's righteousness in Christ stands on the solid ground of the intentions he established at creation (Q & A 6) and in the covenant he made with Israel (Q & A 19). If justifying the unrighteous were opposed to his former intentions and claims, then God would be unfaithful and unjust. But in Jesus, God is faithful not only to his creatures but to himself. In Jesus, God fulfills creation and covenant. God the redeemer is also God the creator and judge. So our response to God the redeemer does not deliver us from our responsibilities to God the creator and judge; on the contrary, it holds us to them. That should keep us from so spiritualizing the righteousness of God the redeemer that we exile it to an other-world, rendering it irrelevant to this world God created or to the social righteousness God covenanted.

In Jesus, God's righteousness is our righteousness. The prophet's name for Jesus was "The Lord is our righteousness" (Jeremiah 23:6, referred to by Q & A 19) and this righteousness—the Messiah, our righteousness—"executes justice and righteousness in the land" (Jer. 23:5). If we abandon either the creation or the social hopes of the "old covenant," then we cannot own the righteousness of God, the Christ promised by the prophets and enfleshed in Jesus. Then, instead, we worship a Christ of our own imagination, and the righteousness of God is far from us. If he is our righteousness, then he is our social righteousness too. "For our sake he made him to be sin who knew no sin, so that in him we might become the righteousness of God" (2 Cor. 5:21, referred to by Qs & As 15 and 17).

In this sad world a faithful response to God the redeemer will not and cannot disown this world that God created or the social righteousness God covenanted. In this sad world a faithful response to God the redeemer will and must own responsibility for God's righteousness and for the work of reconciliation. "All this is from God, who through Christ reconciled us to himself and gave us the ministry of reconciliation" (2 Cor. 5:18). So when, in this sad world, the dignity and equality and unity of persons are broken and trampled by sin, when hunger endangers little children, when injustice and oppression threaten a neighbor, when wars alarm and promise chaos—then we are a people possessed by God's righteousness, given a ministry of reconciliation, and responsible to God in and for his world.

Psalm 8 and Responsibility

In its Old Testament setting, Psalm 8 is a hymn of praise. The psalmist is gripped by the vastness of God's creation, awed by the magnificence of the heavens, overwhelmed by the stunning creative power of God. His spontaneous reaction is "What is man that thou art mindful of him, and the son of man that thou dost care for him?" (v. 4). The psalmist's sense of human insignificance in the midst of the splendor of God's creation does not, however, pass into indolence (as is all too typically human). Instead, the psalmist moves on to confess that God has made his human creatures "little less than God" (v. 5) and given them dominion over the creation (v. 6). Here is no simple tribute to humanity, no mere praise of the creation itself, but rather a hymn of praise to God the creator: "O Lord, our Lord, how majestic is thy name in all the earth!" (vv. 1, 9). And in this hymn of praise people accept their responsibility to exercise their dominion under God, to respond faithfully to God the creator so that the whole creation might flourish by human powers, not languish because of them.

Psalm 8 is frequently quoted in the New Testament, but most extensively in Hebrews 2:6–8 (see also Eph. 1:22, 1 Cor. 15:27, Matt. 21:16, and parallels). Here the tension is no longer between human insignificance and our office as lords of creation; here the tension arises from the obvious fact that we are not in control of this world. "As it is," the writer of Hebrews says, "we do not yet see everything in subjection to him" (v. 8). The actual state of humanity is not the role graciously given and commanded by God. The actual state of humanity is rather the fallen state of bondage and helplessness. People are estranged from God's intended blessing and responsibility. They have floundered and are lost. It's a sad world. "But," the writer continues, "we see Jesus." Psalm 8 is true of him. He "for a little while was made lower than the angels" and is "crowned with glory and honor" (v. 9). Hebrews 2 and the other New Testament passages read Psalm 8 as a reference to Christ.

In its plain sense, of course, Psalm 8 speaks of humanity. It is humanity to whom God has subjected the creation; in fact, that's one cause of the psalmist's amazement. But that doesn't mean the exegesis of Hebrews is wrong. The writer of Hebrews has not left behind the natural reading for one that serves his purpose. He does not deny that the Psalm refers to humanity, but rather elaborates on that interpretation: Christ is the new humanity. He is the "truly human and truly righteous" one who establishes God's righteousness and our own. In him the righteousness of the creator and covenanter are fulfilled. In him we are restored to "righteousness and life." The corruption that threatens the creation and divides humanity has its remedy in him. In him we are no longer in bondage to that corruption; we are restored to the position of Psalm 8, to exercising responsibility to God in and for his creation. Psalm 8 is true of both Christ and us, but it is true of us only because it is true of Christ. Christ is the truly human, the second and life-giving Adam, the new humanity.

To own his righteousness as our righteousness is not to disown human responsibility in this world, but to be restored to it, renewed for it. It is to "put on the new nature, which is being renewed in knowledge after the image of its creator. Here there cannot be Greek and Jew, circumcised and uncircumcised, barbarian, Scythian, slave, free man, but Christ is all, and in all" (Col. 3:10, 11).

Race and Responsibility

Our responsibility to God as creator, judge, and redeemer profoundly illuminates our responsibilities in many modern problems, and certainly not least of all in race relations. The racial problem no longer receives quite the attention it did a decade and a half ago, and we are sometimes tempted to think that the problems now are purely technical ones or, at the worst, moral inertia. We are tempted to think that our society and the church are no longer prejudiced, that it merely takes time to change institutions created over four hundred years.

Those who own the catechism as a standard certainly applaud recognition of human unity and equality. But the moral realism of the catechism forces us to go deeper. It prompts the question of whether delays in accomplishing admittedly high goals can be accounted for simply as technical problems beyond our control.

The problem of racism has never been fundamentally a technical problem; it has always been a moral and religious problem. The problem of racism is our failure to act faithfully in response to God the creator, judge, and redeemer. All the other problems revolve around this incorrigible irresponsibility of ours.

We can begin with creation. "God created man good and in his own image" (Q & A 6). In 1900 a book entitled *The Negro a Beast* was published by the American Book and Bible Society. To convince its readers of the "biblical truths" presented in the book, the author included pictures of God, white men, and black men. The pictures made it very clear that the white man alone was made in the image of God and that the black man was "simply a beast without a soul." The book had a wide circulation—mainly, of course, among white, church-going males.

The absurdity of that book and its claims should strike anyone who reads them. God is not white and certainly not a white racist. God is no color (black?), and his image is no color.

The biblical accounts of creation are unique in many ways. For example, Genesis 1 and 2 give us the story of man, of *ha-Adam*. Other creation accounts present stories about the original ancestors of a particular tribe or nation or race. Genesis 1 and 2 have none of that. They are not tribal or national or racial stories. They do not exalt one set of people above all others. They announce the unity of the human family.

Christians often get involved in heated discussions about Genesis 1 and 2. We all want to keep faith with these stories, and we spend a lot of time arguing about what is important in this part of Scripture. Many of the arguments, however, sadly ignore the message of the unity of the human family.

The challenge that Genesis 1 and 2 bring to the faithful today is not so much to affirm and defend the very fact that a firmament divided the waters above the earth from the waters below the earth. It is rather to affirm and defend the view that there is a family that unites the whites and the blacks, browns, reds, and yellows, and . . . every nation on all the face of the earth. Perhaps we are not as ludicrous in our denials as that book with pictures of God. But every time we accept and affirm political and social and economic policies that effectively deny the unity of the human family, we fail to keep faith with the story of God's creation, fail to respond in faith to God the creator.

In Athens, Paul stood before the Greeks, to whom others were "barbarians" with strange languages, and courageously announced the unity of the human family in creation: "He made from one every nation of men to live on all the face of the earth" (Acts 17:26). May we be less courageous in the presence of racial slurs? Not if we are to respond faithfully to God the creator.

The issues, of course, go deeper than name-calling. We respond to God the creator in politics and economics—and evangelism! Paul's evangelism did not sidestep the unity of the human family for fear of causing offense. Nor should ours. Formulas for "church growth along socially homogeneous lines" must be carefully examined and qualified or dismissed in the light of our responsibility to God the creator. Evangelism is the task of the church in faithfulness to God, but if it sustains and nurtures divisions in the human family, then even evangelism can fail to keep faith with God the creator. Paul's churches reflected the renewal of creation, where "there cannot be Greek and Jew, circumcised and uncircumcised, barbarian, Scythian, slave, free man" (Col. 3:11). And so should ours.

The catechism knows that because people have fallen, departures from unity and equity can be expected; but it never teaches that such departures may be condoned or encouraged. The enmity and inequities among us are a part of our corruption. The parasite of our reckless disobedience here festers in the sores of a racist past. Like the catechism says, the sins of our parents have "poisoned our nature" (Q & A 7). Sin captures us and makes us slaves.

Here I can only speak of and for my own race. Most of us white Christians pride ourselves on having disowned racism. We can get quite indignant about apartheid, and properly so; but at the same time we quietly give our assent to a racist past by doing nothing to change practices of hiring, firing, training, locating, and so forth. The sin of racism has poisoned our nature so that, while few of us are overtly prejudiced, we still, in effect, discriminate against other races.

Even our concern is tainted by paternalism: we show kindness to others within centuries-old structures of inequity and injustice. We twist "I am indeed my brother's keeper" until "keeper" becomes a despicable word. We love our neighbor not according to the pattern of unity and equity given by God, but rather according to the pattern of transactions accepted in our culture's heritage—and then only as long as our neighbor understands and keeps "his place."

We have fallen from the blessing and responsibility given by God the creator. "Will God permit such disobedience and rebellion to go unpunished? Certainly not. He is terribly angry about the sin we are born with as well as the sins we personally commit" (Q & A 10). God encounters us as judge of our racism and demands that we respond faithfully to him. Such a faithful response involves both contrition and change. Contrition means I acknowledge that I need the admonition also of my brothers and sisters who are of a different race. I need to be open to their judgment and ready to say "I'm sorry."

Such contrition can lead to change, and change is always part of a faithful response to God the judge. Change means committing oneself to the rightness of God's verdict and working for political institutions, economic policies, social relationships, and church policy which image that verdict.

So we are responsible to God the creator and the judge in race relations. The really remarkable thing, however, is that God is our redeemer. He does not redeem us by tolerating sin. God's mercy does not compromise with racism; he will not let go either of his own righteousness or of us. So he does not free us *from* our responsibilities; he frees us *for* them. He delivers us from our bondage to racism and frees us for the righteousness he gives and claims.

In redemption, God's intentions at creation are fulfilled through a renewed unity of the human family. Jesus Christ is God's righteousness—and ours. "He is our peace, who has made us both one, and has broken down the dividing wall of hostility" (Eph. 2:14). He is the new nature, the new humanity, where there is not Jew and Gentile, Greek or barbarian (Col. 3:11). He is our righteousness, also racially.

We respond to God the redeemer faithfully by putting on the new nature and by taking up the "ministry of reconciliation" (2 Cor. 5:18). As Johannes Verkuyl said, "If it is true that he has broken down the walls between men, then we are conscripted to join the work of demolition." Evangelistic policies of church growth along socially homogeneous and tribal and racial lines put mortar in the walls that divide people when we should be breaking them down. Such evangelism, ironically, makes it more difficult for people to respond faithfully to God the redeemer by putting on the new nature and taking up the ministry of reconciliation.

Note that the ministry of reconciliation does not require uniformity. Jewish Christians and Gentile Christians in the early church were not required to give up their Jewish or Gentile identities. But they were required to be one community of Jew and Gentile; they were required not to judge or despise one another but to welcome and love one another (see Romans 14:1–15:13). Today, too, the model of reconciliation is not assimilation—that is, conformity to "our" customs and culture. But it is surely not a mosaic model, either, where colors dwell side by side without touching or influencing each other. The model is reconciliation; if we are to be the church, the image of a renewed creation, a new nature, we recognize the need for others who are different from us.

We are a denomination of many races. God the creator, judge, and redeemer has been at work among us. But we have to respond faithfully to him. Demanding that everyone conform to "our" (Dutch or Scotch or Italian or . . .) ethnic heritage or demanding that anyone renounce "their" ethnic heritage is not a faithful response. Being content with a mosaic of colors and races that seldom touch or influence each other is not a faithful response either. We need to touch each other, to overcome the sense of alienation from one another. We need to work together on issues of justice. We need to admonish and encourage one another. We need to tell and to hear the old, old stories of slavery and prejudice and discrimination and to connect those stories with their lingering and festering social effects. But, above all, we need to tell and live the stories of creation and judgment and deliverance.

Acknowledgments and Suggestions for Further Reading

The quotation from Lewis Smedes at the opening of the chapter is from *Mere Morality* (Grand Rapids: Wm. B. Eerdmans, 1983), p. 34. This book, which treats love, justice, and the commands of the second table of the Decalogue, is very valuable for anyone concerned with Reformed theological ethics.

The notion of "responsibility" is central to the work of H. R. Niebuhr, *The Responsible Self: An Essay in Christian Moral Philosophy* (New York: Harper & Row, 1963). That book has been the single most influential book in Christian ethics in this century. Among the work it influenced is Waldo Beach, *The Christian Life* (Richmond: The Covenant Life Curriculum Press, 1966). Pages 232–257 of Beach's book influenced this chapter significantly.

On Psalm 8 see Brevard Childs, *Biblical Theology in Crisis* (Philadelphia: Westminster Press, 1970), pp. 151–163.

On the use of Psalm 8 in Hebrews see C. K. Barrett, "The Eschatology of the Epistle to the Hebrews" in W. D. Davies and D. Daube, eds., *The Background of the New Testament and Its Eschatology* (Cambridge: Cambridge University Press, 1964), p. 391.

The quote from Johannes Verkuyl comes from *Break Down the Walls: A Christian Cry for Racial Justice*, translated by Lewis Smedes (Grand Rapids: Wm. B. Eerdmans, 1973), p.12. On racism see further the "Declarations on Race" in *Acts of Synod 1968*, pp. 17ff.

The evangelism policy "church growth along socially homogeneous lines" is part of the recommendations of the church growth movement created by Donald McGavran. His successor, C. Peter Wagner, has written a book outlining the movement's methodologies and objectives, entitled (revealingly) *Our Kind of People* (Atlanta: John Knox Press, 1979). For a view of evangelism that keeps faith with the Heidelberg Catechism, see Richard Mouw, *Political Evangelism* (Grand Rapids: Wm. B. Eerdmans, 1973).

Discussion Questions for Chapter 4

1. Read Ephesians 2:11–22. Try to imagine the reaction of Jewish Christians and Gentile Christians. Remember the enmity between Jew and Gentile was strong. The Jewish revolutionary war began in A.D. 66, and anti-Semitic feeling flashed into race riots in a number of Hellenistic cities.

   What is "the dividing wall" of verse 14? Were the Gentiles later assimilated into Jewish culture and customs? Were they required, for example, to be circumcised? Were the Jews assimilated into Gentile customs? Were they forbidden, for example, to keep kosher, to observe the sabbath, to circumcise their sons? What does it mean to be "one" in Jesus Christ?

Now try to paraphrase Ephesians 2:11–22 so that it speaks to your church in the twentieth century. Who are the Jews? The Gentiles? What walls divide people from one another today? How are they broken down? How does your church image the "one new man in place of the two"?

2. Do you agree that "church growth along socially homogeneous lines" is not an acceptable normative principle for evangelism? Why or why not? Does your evangelism program include a concern for those who are not "your kind" of people? What do you do to invite them and to welcome them?

3. Does your church have regular and meaningful contact with other Christians who are not like you, who are of another race or class? Do you? Why is such contact important if we are to respond in faith to God the creator? Or to God the judge? Or to God the redeemer?

4. Since the Supreme Court decision requiring integration of public schools, a lot of Christian academies and Christian schools have been started. Many of them are segregated. What special responsibilities do Christian schools have for enabling students to respond in faith to God in all areas, including that of race relations? Can Christian schools really fulfill those responsibilities if they do not include children of other races? How important is it for children to experience the humanity of other children who are "not like them?" Are scholarship programs for minorities to attend Christian schools a good thing? Why or why not?

5. What do you intend to *do* differently (or more intensely) as a result of having studied and discussed this section of the catechism?

5

Believing In God The Father Almighty

Q. What do you believe when you say:
  "I believe in God the Father, almighty,
  maker of heaven and earth"?

A. That the eternal Father of our Lord Jesus Christ,
    who out of nothing created heaven and earth
      and everything in them,
    who still upholds and rules them
      by his eternal counsel and providence,
  is my God and Father
    because of Christ his Son.

  I trust him so much that I do not doubt
    he will provide
      whatever I need
      for body and soul,
    and he will turn to my good
      whatever adversity he sends me
      in this sad world.

  He is able to do this because he is almighty God;
  he desires to do this because he is a faithful Father.
                          —Heidelberg Catechism Q & A 26

Q. What do you understand
by the providence of God?

A. Providence is
    the almighty and ever present power of God
      by which he upholds, as with his hand,
        heaven
        and earth
        and all creatures,
     and so rules them that
      leaf and blade,
      rain and drought,
      fruitful and lean years,
      food and drink,
      health and sickness,
      prosperity and poverty—
     all things, in fact, come to us
      not by chance
      but from his fatherly hand.
                          —Heidelberg Catechism Q & A 27

Q. How does the knowledge
of God's creation and providence
help us?

A. We can be patient when things go against us,
    thankful when things go well,
    and for the future we can have
    good confidence in our faithful God and Father
    that nothing will separate us from his love.
    All creatures are so completely in his hand
      that without his will
      they can neither move nor be moved.
                  —Heidelberg Catechism Q & A 28

And God saw everything that he had made, and behold, it was very good.
                              —Genesis 1:31a

The earth is the Lord's and the fulness thereof.
                              —Psalm 24:1a

The earth he has given to the sons of men.
                              —Psalm 115:16

The creation waits with eager longing for the revealing of the sons of God.
—Romans 8:19

Calvin, as is well known, everywhere stresses God's ceaseless activity in the world. God is active directly in "the order of nature," where no so-called "natural laws" exist to obstruct the free exercise of his power. He is directly active in "the order of history," where, through general and special providences, he sets up and puts down men and nations in his determination to secure the ends of love and justice.

—Henry Stob

WITHIN ITS SECTION on deliverence in Christ, the catechism deals with the Apostle's Creed, but not as the basis for mere theological speculation. The catechism is never interested in an abstract theological rationalism divorced from life. It uses every article of the Apostles' Creed as a foundation for the Christian nurture of the whole person and the community.

The catechism's treatment of the first article of the Apostles' Creed is a compelling example of how the Heidelberg permits no divorce between creed and life. The question is, What do you believe when you say: "I believe in God the Father, almighty, maker of heaven and earth"? And the answer is a theological gem:

That the eternal Father of our Lord Jesus Christ,
*   who out of nothing created heaven and earth*
*   and everything in them,*
*   who still upholds and rules them*
*   by his eternal counsel and providence,*
is my God and Father
*   because of Christ his Son.*

I trust him so much that I do not doubt
*   he will provide*
*   whatever I need*
*   for body and soul,*
*   and he will turn to my good*
*   whatever adversity he sends me*
*   in this sad world.*

He is able to do this because he is almighty God;
he desires to do this because he is a faithful Father.

Different facets of this gem will capture our attention in this chapter.

The Father of Our Lord Jesus Christ

The catechism's confession about the Father is no intrusion into its confession about the deliverance wrought in Christ. It is the "Father of our Lord Jesus Christ" who is the creator and preserver of this world. And it is in Jesus Christ that we may be sure the creator and preserver of this world intends our good. The catechism allows no divorce between the Father and the Son, between our creation and our redemption.

It permits no truck with Marcion, that second-century heretic who insisted that the god who created this world was the enemy both of humanity and of the God who sent Jesus Christ as our deliverer. According to Marcion, "this sad world" is the work of the creator God worshiped by the Jews and revealed in the Old Testament. Jesus was sent by another God, a redeemer God, to rescue us from "this sad world" and from the influence of its god. According to Marcion, Christians have to repudiate and reject "this sad world."

Before long, the Christian church saw that it had to repudiate and reject Marcion's views. Church leaders excommunicated Marcion in A.D. 144 and took some important positive steps to counter his influence. First, the church affirmed that Christians believe in God the Father, almighty, maker of heaven and earth. Second, it insisted that the Old Testament was authoritative for Christians as well as Jews. And third, it began to collect and canonize a New Testament. Even so, the church continued (and continues) to be threatened by the kind of otherworldly theology that can only enable and require rejection of "this sad world."

The catechism sides with the ancient church in rejecting Marcion and insisting that the creator and preserver of this world is the same God as the Father of our Lord Jesus Christ.

Because this is so, faith in Jesus Christ binds us in loyalty to the maker and upholder of this world.

Because this is so, faith in Jesus enables and requires the costly comfort which acknowledges that we are stewards of this sad world and agents for its reclamation.

Because this is so, the deliverance wrought by God in Jesus Christ is connected inseparably to this real and sad world, to our mundane existence, to our fleshly life with all its organic and contractual relationships—even as these extend to social, economic, and political spheres of life.

The catechism thus protects the church from otherworldliness. It warns us against any spirituality that contemplates rejection of and rescue from this sad world. And it calls us to a joyful, confident, and costly loyalty to the creator and upholder of this world. Loyalty to him will have consequences in this sad world.

God the Creator

The Heidelberg Catechism joins the ancient church in confessing that God "out of nothing created heaven and earth and everything in them" (Q & A 26). That is a simple confession—and easily memorized—but its consequences for the world are profound.

The creed's confession that God made all things out of nothing was directed initially against two alternative views about the source of all things.

Some thought that there were finally two sources of whatever exists—one bad and one good. Gnostic dualists, for example, said that the soul was good because it had a good source but that the body was evil because it had an evil source. To them the church said, "No. God made all things out of nothing, and, therefore, all God made is good."

Others thought that all things were not so much made by God as they flowed from God. All things were, then, in some sense, God himself. But to this group too—to the pantheists—the church said, "No. God made all things out of nothing, and therefore, nothing God made is god."

The simple confession of the catechism, then, demands that we say both "All God made is good" and "Nothing God made is god."

Even though few of us know dualists or pantheists, this confession remains vital. Perhaps we are not in much danger in our sex-oriented society of thinking of the body as evil, but we may have the tendency to make the body a god. All that God made is good, but nothing God made is god.

We are not in much danger in our consumer society of treating falcons or tigers or trees or leopards as gods, but we may fail to treat them as good. Nothing God made is god, but all that God made is good.

In George Orwell's little book *Animal Farm* the pigs continually chant a slogan: "Four legs good, two legs bad." Those who lived in New Testament times had similar chants: "Jew good, Gentile bad" and "Gentile good, Jew bad." The racist slogans are not yet silenced in our world, but the confession of the church that God "out of nothing created heaven and earth and everything in them" continues to oppose all racism. All that God made is good, and nothing God made is god.

It is possible, of course, and even important to ask whether we really believe this confession. Is all that God made really good? The counter-evidence seems to surround us: wars, famine, injustice, and even such prosaic things as petty, quarrelsome people and hard, dreary work. But neither the Bible nor the catechism denies that there is evil in the world. What the Bible says, and says flatly, is that God made all things and that he made all things *good*. "God saw everything that he had made, and behold, it was very good" (Gen. 1:31a). The warnings of the Bible are never directed against God's creation but against our misuse of it, against human sin. The "almighty God" is a "faithful Father" (Q & A 26). He can be trusted and he is to be praised.

The catechism's confession, like all good theology, leads to doxology. All good, clear-headed thinking about God must finally become praise of God. And all good doxology leads to Christian living, for God is praised, above all, in lives that are patient and thankful and confident (Q & A 28).

So praise him. Praise him for all that he has made, for "all things bright and beautiful, all creatures great and small." As Gerard Manley Hopkins said in his poem, "Pied Beauty,"

Glory be to God for dappled things— . . .
All things counter, original, spare, strange; . . .
He fathers-forth whose beauty is past change:
Praise him.

Crocuses and bodies he fathers-forth whose beauty is past change. The variety of the human race—black, red, pale—he fathers-forth. The magnificent assortment of the gifts and skills of others on whom we depend he fathers-forth. So praise him, for all is good and all is God's. And live in praise, owning the confession of the catechism. Live in gratitude.

Receive and delight in a summer evening or a spring day. They are not to be worshiped, but they are good. Protect and care for God's world in all its "pied beauty."

Receive and delight in your parents. They are not gods, but they are good. "Be patient with their failings—for through them God chooses to rule" you (Q & A 104).

Receive and delight in every human heart that beats alongside your own. Love your neighbors; "be patient, peace-loving, gentle, merciful, and friendly" to them (Q & A 107).

Receive and delight in your bodies. They are good—not to be worshiped, but they are good. Delight in them, then, as persons who recognize that they are not gods but God's, "temples of the Holy Spirit" (Q & A 109).

You may even receive and delight in your possessions. Things can tempt us to worship them, but they are good. Receive them, then, and delight in them as stewards, as people who are responsible to God to "share with those in need" (Q & A 111).

God the Provider

God did not just create the world and then leave it to run like some well-oiled piece of machinery. He did not just create it and then leave it to be destroyed by that parasite evil. God cares for his world. He sustains it. He restrains the effects of sin upon it. He still "upholds and rules" it.

A fair paraphrase for the catechism's thought is that God's care is the world's constant companion. That thought has its classic expression in the doctrine of providence and has been part of the church's thought from the very beginning. So the catechism joins the ancient church in confessing God's providence and rejecting both chance and fate as the explanation of our lives. "All things, in fact, come to us," the catechism says, not by chance or by fate, "but from his fatherly hand" (Q & A 27).

The ancient Epicureans thought all things happened by chance. According to that line of thinking there is no meaning, no justice, no purpose in the world or in history; there is just chance. So to the Epicureans it made sense to live by a simple motto: Eat, drink, and be merry, for tomorrow we die. But to them—and to all our contemporaries who think life is meaningless and history pointless—the ancient church and the catechism and a social ethic faithful to the catechism say, "No. All things come to us not by chance but from his fatherly hand. He upholds and rules the world for the sake of the same loving intentions with which he created the world. God's care is the world's constant companion."

Others—the ancient Stoics, for example—thought all things were determined by fate. To the Stoics, people are merely puppets in the hands of necessity. No human action can affect history, and any human resolve is powerless against the strength of fate. So to the stoics it made sense not to get angry with evil or delight too much in the good. To them, too, and to all our contemporaries who urge apathy and indifference and a death to passion—the ancient church and the catechism and a social ethic faithful to the catechism say, "No. All things come to us not by fate but from his fatherly hand. He upholds and rules all things for the sake of the same project of human freedom and fruition with which he began the world. God's care is the world's constant companion."

All things are ruled not by chance, not by fate, but by God's fatherly hand. God will not allow sin to have the final word in his world. His care is the world's constant companion.

Again, we must ask whether we can and do really believe this confession. The truth about our sad world is dripping with blood. The truth about our world hangs on a cross. Disease and death, poverty and pain, war and rumors of war—that's the truth about our world. Our comfort may not (and does not) make liars of us. The tyrant jokes on his way to work. And marriages fail. Everyone knows these things. And as usual the cynics are at least more honest than the romantics who think that every life ends in a sunset on a broad cinemascope screen and that every social intention ends in utopia.

Miracles are at best a random lot. And though God's care is the world's constant companion, he seldom runs to save the milk from spilling or eases the guilty conscience of an affluent society. The parasite evil causes pain and the physician's care is sometimes painful too. God's providence includes his judgment. He seldom runs to save.

53

But save he does. He saves through our Lord Jesus Christ. It was in the cross that we saw the world's greatest evil. It is also there that we see the world's greatest good. God's care is the world's constant companion. God's care is the constant companion of the very world that stands against him. God's care is the constant companion of the very world that nailed his Son to a tree. God's care is the constant companion of even this cynic's world. The cross is no lie, either as a revelation of human sin or as the revelation of divine love. God's care is the world's constant companion.

Again the catechism's confession leads us to praise. So praise him. Praise him for the meaning in life, for all things come not by chance. Praise him for the freedom in life, for all things happen not by fate. Praise him in joy. Praise him in sadness. Praise him for the presence of his care in a thunderstorm and for the promise of his care in a rainbow. Praise him for the truth, even the truth that hurts. Praise him for the cross. "Praise him, praise him, all ye little children, God is love," and his love is our constant companion.

Again the point of the catechism is that he is to be praised above all in lives of patience, thankfulness, and confidence (Q & A 28). We must live our lives in the presence and promise of God's care.

We may not be indifferent or passive about the evil that infects our lives and our common, political, social, economic, and ecclesiastical life. On the contrary, we may and must make God's intentions our intentions, God's passions our passions. It is God's fatherly hand that rules, after all, not fate. And we may not allow that parasite evil the last word in God's world. We may not simply eat, drink, and be merry. On the contrary, to praise God for the cross is to take up the cross. And to take up the cross is to take up the suffering and long-suffering love of God, the love that suffers others' hurts and weeps with those who weep. It is God's fatherly hand that upholds, after all, not chance; and we may not allow that parasite evil the last word in God's world.

To praise God in sadness is to "be patient when things go against us" (Q & A 28). To praise him for the truth is to "love the truth, speak it candidly, and openly acknowledge it" (Q &A 112). To praise him for his love is to live in "good confidence in our faithful God and Father" (Q & A 28), to have the courage of our comfort, and boldly and confidently to refuse that parasite evil the last word in God's world or our common life.

The catechism's confession of God's providence demands a final caution. As Hendrikus Berkhof warns, we face "the danger of a kind of belief in providence which can create social quietism and make the church indulgent in injustice and social inequities." We must be careful lest we slip back into fatalism. God does not remove our freedom by his providence; he preserves it. He does not destroy our humanity by his providence; he sustains it. Our freedom and full humanity are a part of God's intention, and he governs with that intention always in view.

In this world the confession that "all things . . . come to us . . . from his fatherly hand" (Q & A 27) will often have an "in spite of" attached. *In spite of* the agony of Christ's death, we believe God's care and loving intentions are present. *In spite of* sickness, we believe God's care and healing purpose are present. *In spite of* oppression and hunger and poverty, we believe God's care and his cause of justice are present. *In spite of* sin and evil, we believe God's care is our constant companion and the world's constant companion.

We sometimes talk as though death, sickness, oppression, poverty, war, sin, and evil were themselves God's intentions. No! If we are to stop withstanding God and stand with God, if we are to be God's companions as he is our companion, if we are to live in the praise of God, then we may never stand with any posture other than hatred toward death and sickness and oppression and poverty and war and sin and evil.

Providence does not call us to become passionless. It calls us to share in Christ's passion. He has fought with sin and death—and he has won. So we return to the initial and most important observation. The God who creates and preserves this world is the "Father of our Lord Jesus Christ" (Q & A 26). He is toward us in creation and in providence as he is toward us in Jesus Christ. And he calls us in creating and preserving as he calls us in Jesus Christ to a life of patient love (which is not apathy about sickness, poverty, or evil), thankful service (which is not complacency with the social status quo), and confidence (which is neither despair nor presumption). "Looking to our crucified and risen Lord, we may confess concerning the totality of our ambiguous situation that it comes to us by God's fatherly hand and that in everything he works for good with those who love him."

Faith and the Earth

The church that confesses the catechism binds itself in loyalty to the creator and preserver of this world. That statement has manifold implications, some of which we have hinted at in the previous section. For the moment we will concentrate on the implications of the catechism for the use of natural resources.

In a widely read essay, Lynn White places heavy blame on Christianity for the ecological crisis. He says, "Our science and technology have grown out of Christian attitudes toward man's relation to nature. . . . We are superior to nature, contemptuous of it, willing to use it for our slightest whim. . . ."

It is difficult to disagree entirely with White's placement of responsibility. Christianity must accept some share of the responsibility for the ecological crisis. And we are only nit-picking if we debate how big a share of the blame it must accept.

More to the point than Christianity's share of the blame in the past is its ability to respond now. As Lynn White says, "Since the roots of our trouble are so largely religious, the remedy must also be essentially religious, whether we call it that or not." Jorgen Randers of MIT agrees: "Probably only religion has the moral force to bring such a change" in our attitude toward nature and our relation to it. Some ecologists have so little confidence that Christianity will respond to the crisis in a helpful way that they are looking elsewhere for religious remedies—particularly to pantheism, which (it is thought) motivates an awesome reverence for all of nature.

But Christians must respond. That is why the catechism reminds us of our responsibility and offers resources to heal our antagonism toward nature: The Father of our Lord Jesus Christ is the creator and preserver of this world. All things that he made are good. His care is the world's constant companion. We must live in loyalty to him. We are responsible to him for our world and its ecosystem.

Because of the rapid expansion of human power, we are especially tempted to sunder this doctrine from life, to turn the confession that all is God's into a pious irrelevancy. Human technology, our ability to control nature, has outrun the wildest dreams of earlier generations. At the same time our sense of our own importance dwindles as our knowledge of nature expands. And so Pascal's paradox that human grandeur is human misery and human misery is human grandeur is a still harsher truth today. This magnificent and pathetic creature, the human being, both needs a sense of belonging to something or someone absolutely trustworthy; and prides himself, thanks to his remarkable science and technology, on being the creator and provider sufficient to himself.

It is precisely here, then, that the catechism's confession can indeed tell us something important about us and our life on the earth. It tells us of the dominion of an absolutely trustworthy God and would have us exercise our human dominion under him. That makes our dominion a responsible dominion, an answerable and accountable dominion. It is not that dominion is taken from humanity (cf. Gen. 1:26–28). It is rather that human beings are numbered with God's other creatures and thus are accountable in their dominion to God the Father of our Lord Jesus Christ, the creator and owner of all.

Such dominion will stand in lively contrast to the technological enthusiasm of many in our culture, enthusiasm like that exhibited by Kingsley Davis in celebration of the conquest and control of human genes. "Deliberate control," he says, "would soon benefit science and technology, which in turn would facilitate further hereditary improvement, which again would extend science, and so on in a self-reinforcing spiral without limit. In other words, when man has conquered his own biological evolution, he will have laid the basis for conquering everything else. The universe will be his at last."

A dominion that keeps faith with the catechism, I suggest, will be more care-taking than conquering, more nurturing than controlling, more ready to suffer patiently with nature than to lord it over and against nature. A dominion that answers to God will acknowledge humbly that we are only creatures ourselves, and as fallible as finite, ultimately dependent on the creator and on the creation he has put in our care. A dominion that responds in faith to God will own responsibility for the well-being of the whole creation.

The doctrine of the catechism is no inane sentimentality. But it may look like such and become such if the church does not live by it, if the church does not call human dominion to responsibility, if the church does not have the courage of her comfort to condemn human rapacity. The church must make God's creative passion her own and be an advocate for egrets, peregrine falcons, and grizzlies. All that God made is good.

Are these ecological issues any of the church's business? If the confession is the church's charter, then advocating for ecology is certainly the church's business. Indeed the credibility of our confession is at stake in our willingness to make such advocacy our business. We can view Lord's Day 9 and 10 as inane sentimentality or we can receive them as vital truth.

The church can call human dominion to responsibility simply on the basis of prudence. Human beings are, after all, a part of creation, a part of this ecosystem, and its destruction is their destruction, its abasement is their abasement. But the horror stories, the barrage of scientific accounts of the disasters befalling water and land and air, apparently are not suffi-cient to call us to responsibility. Surely our fears can motivate us, our guilt and our anxiety for generations yet unborn (if they are to be born). But the church can and must proclaim "a more excellent way", a vision of humanity restored to a responsible dominion over that which God created good.

And that is the hope of nature too. "The creation waits with eager longing for the revealing of the sons of God" (Rom. 8:19). God made, pre-serves, and redeems this earth. When he raised Jesus from the dead, he sealed this world's destiny. His intentions in creation will be victorious. Evil is not the final word in his creation any more than it is the first word. Humanity's rapacity is neither the first account of human dominion nor the final account. The lines between the confession that God the Father of our Lord Jesus Christ is this world's creator and preserver and our everyday life on this planet cannot be drawn too boldly.

The performatory consequence of the honest affirmations that all that God made is good and that God's care is the world's constant compan-ion is our own constant and responsible care for the earth and its creatures.

Acknowledgments and Suggestions for Further Reading

The quote from Henry Stob at the beginnning of the chapter is from "God and Man," *Ethical Reflections* (Grand Rapids: Wm. B. Eerdmans, 1978), p. 53.

Langdon Gilkey, *Maker of Heaven and Earth* (Garden City, N.Y.: Doubleday, 1959) is a very perceptive and helpful book.

Gerard Manley Hopkins's poem "Pied Beauty" is found in G.M. Hopkins, *Poems*, 3rd edition (London: Oxford University Press, 1948), p. 74.

The quotations from Hendrikus Berkhof are from his "The Catechism as an Expression of our Faith" in Bard Thomson et al., *Essays on the Heidelberg Catechism* (Philadelphia: United Church Press, 1963), p. 104.

The Lynn White quote is from "The Historical Roots of Our Ecological Crisis," appended to Francis Schaeffer, *Pollution and the Death of Man* (Wheaton, Illinois: Tyndale House, 1970), p.111. The quote from Jorgen Randers is from "Global Limitations and Human Responsibility" in Kenneth Vaux, ed., *To Create a Different Future* (New York: Friendship Press, 1972), p. 32. The quote from Kingsley Davis is from his "Sociological Aspects of Genetic Control" in William Peterson, ed., *Readings in Population* (New York: Macmillan, Inc. 1972), p. 379.

Recommendations for further study of the ecological crisis: Henry Stob, "Christian Ethics and Scientific Control," *Ethical Reflections*, pp. 209–223; Loren Wilkinson, ed., *Earth-Keeping* (Grand Rapids: Wm. B. Eerdmans, 1980). Specifically on the question of genetic engineering, see Allen Verhey, "The Morality of Genetic Engineering," *Christian Scholars' Review* (XIV, 2; 1985), pp. 124–139.

Discussion Questions for Chapter 5

1. A local newspaper reported that a church refused to fix its septic tank even though the tank was proven to cause pollution. In what sense did modern followers of Marcion worship there? Even if we disown Marcion's strange heresy in theory, how can we be guilty of the same kind of "practical heresy" in our attitude toward and use of natural resources?

2. List and then discuss some of the implications for our life of the ancient church's rejection of gnostic dualism, pantheism, epicureanism, and stoicism.

3. Suppose the government plans to build a nuclear power generator plant near your church. Before church on Sunday morning a conversation like the following takes place:

   Abe: I'm worried about the effects of spent fuel rods and radioactive liquid waste on the health of wildlife in the area.

   Barbara: Good grief, you old bunny-lover. The real issue is whether they'd be dangerous to humans.

   Clara: High-level radioactive waste piles up around nuclear plants. It *is* dangerous to animals *and* humans. And disposal of the waste is no trifling matter. Some of the materials remain toxic for thousands of years. What's our responsibility to future generations?

David: I've heard enough about the dangers. The plant will provide jobs and energy, both of which are badly needed.

Ernestine: I've heard enough, period. We're in church now and shouldn't be thinking about such things.

Frank: Yes, and besides, we need to trust the experts.

Just then the pastor interrupts to remind them the worship service is about to begin. The opening hymn is number 374, "This is My Father's World." After church the conversation continues. Join in!

Whom do you agree with and why?

Before responding, you might consider what bearing the Heidelberg Catechism has on this matter. Also, ask yourself whether we can "trust the experts" if they are technological enthusiasts like Kingsley Davis. Does the church have any business talking about such issues? Is Abe's concern irrelevant? David does have a point, doesn't he?

Perhaps your group will find it helpful to think about David's point in terms of some of the categories used earlier to think about war: just cause, last resort, proportionality, and immunity. That is, perhaps we will have to talk more about whether the nuclear plant will provide significant benefits, whether it is the only way (or at least the least risky way) to provide those benefits, whether the harm done might outweigh the benefits (and, if so, whether the effects of the nuclear plant are reversible), and whether the risks of harm are borne by the people (or creatures) who would benefit. The arguments can be difficult, and facts are obviously crucial, but—as in the issue of war—a good deal depends on whether the burden of proof falls on technology or on those who would restrain technology. Perhaps you can talk about how (or if) the catechism is relevant to this question of the burden of proof.

4. If the technology of genetic control makes it possible to design our offspring, to "facilitate further hereditary improvement" (Kingsley Davis), should we do it? What would it mean to keep faith with the catechism when the nature we're dealing with is human nature? What about designing out genetic diseases or retardation? What about designing in strength or intelligence?

5. Almost every area faces some environmental issue: landfill sites, industrial pollution of air/water/soil, acid rain, nuclear power plants, noise pollution, etc. Discuss one such issue which figures prominently in your area's ecology. Talk about the responsibility of the church and its members in this matter. Should the church act as an institution or should reaction be left to individual members? In either case, what practical steps could be taken to meet our responsibility as caretakers of God's world?

6. Reflect on Psalm 8 during the week and use it as a doxology to God the creator.

6

BELIEVING IN JESUS CHRIST THE LORD

Q. *Why is the Son of God called "Jesus"*
   meaning "Savior"?

A. *Because he saves us from our sins.*
      Salvation cannot be found in anyone else;
      it is futile to look for any salvation elsewhere.
                        —Heidelberg Catechism Q & A 29

Q. *Do those who look for*
   their salvation and security
   in saints, in themselves, or elsewhere
   really believe in the only Savior Jesus?

A. *No.*
   Although they boast of being his,
   by their deeds they deny
   the only savior and deliverer, Jesus.

   Either Jesus is not a perfect savior,
   or those who in true faith accept this savior
   have in him all they need for their salvation.
                        —Heidelberg Catechism Q & A 30

Q. *Why is he called "Christ"*
   meaning "anointed"?

A. *Because he has been ordained by God the Father*
and has been anointed with the Holy Spirit
> *to be*
>> *our chief prophet and teacher*
>>> *who perfectly reveals to us*
>>> *the secret counsel and will of God for our deliverance;*
>> *our only high priest*
>>> *who has set us free by the one sacrifice of his body,*
>>> *and who continually pleads our cause with the Father;*
>> *and our eternal king*
>>> *who governs us by his Word and Spirit,*
>>> *and who guards us and keeps us*
>>> *in the freedom he has won for us.*
>>>>>>> —*Heidelberg Catechism Q & A 31*

Q. *But why are you called a Christian?*

A. *Because by faith I am a member of Christ*
and so I share in his anointing.
> *I am anointed*
>> *to confess his name,*
>> *to present myself to him as a living sacrifice of thanks,*
>> *to strive with a good conscience against sin and the devil in this life,*
>> *and afterward to reign with Christ*
>>> *over all creation*
>>> *for all eternity.*
>>>>>>> —*Heidelberg Catechism Q & A 32*

Q. *Why do you call him "Our Lord"?*

A. *Because—*
> *not with gold or silver,*
> *but with his precious blood—*
he has set us free
> *from sin and from the tyranny of the devil,*
and has bought us,
> *body and soul,*
to be his very own.
>>>>>>> —*Heidelberg Catechism Q & A 34*

As therefore you received Christ Jesus the Lord, so live in him.
>>>>>>> —*Colossians 2:6*

And Mary said, "My soul magnifies the Lord, and my spirit rejoices in God my Savior, for he has regarded the low estate of his handmaiden. For behold, henceforth all generations will call me blessed; for he who is mighty has done great things for me, and holy is his name. And his mercy is on those who fear him from generation to generation. He has shown strength with his arm, he has scattered the proud in the imagination of their hearts, he has put down the mighty from their thrones, and exalted those of low degree; he has filled the hungry with good things, and the rich he has sent empty away."

—Luke 1:46–53

"The Spirit of the Lord is upon me, because he has anointed me to preach good news to the poor. He has sent me to proclaim release to the captives and recovering of sight to the blind, to set at liberty those who are oppressed, to proclaim the acceptable year of the Lord."

—Luke 4:18–19 (Isaiah 61:1–2)

Lead on, O King Eternal,
the day of march has come;
henceforth in fields of conquest
thy tents shall be our home.
Through days of preparation
thy grace has made us strong,
and now, O King Eternal,
we lift our battle song.

Lead on, O King Eternal,
till sin's fierce war shall cease,
and holiness shall whisper
the sweet amen of peace;
for not with swords' loud clashing,
or roll of stirring drums,
with deeds of love and mercy
the heavenly kingdom comes.

Lead on, O King Eternal,
we follow, not with fears;
for gladness breaks like morning
where'er thy face appears;
Thy cross is lifted o'er us,
we journey in its light;
the crown awaits the conquest;
lead on, O God of might.

—"Lead On, O King Eternal"

God the Father, as he has reconciled us to himself in his Christ, has in him stamped for us the likeness to which he would have us conform.

—John Calvin, Institutes, *3, vi, 3*

"LET ALL THE HOUSE Of ISRAEL therefore know assuredly that God has made him both Lord and Christ, this Jesus whom you crucified" (Acts 2:36). In those words Peter concluded his Pentecost sermon. Many people who heard it understood well the connection between doctrine and life; they asked, "What shall we do?" (Acts 2:37). Peter's proclamation—Jesus is Lord—became the early church's first creed and later found expression in the second article of the Apostles' Creed.

The Heidelberg Catechism also understands well the connection between doctrine and life. It celebrates the grace of God in Jesus Christ the Lord, both as the mercy of God upon our lives and as the will of God for our lives—both as grace and as claim. The catechism will permit no divorce of grace from claim in the interest of some cheap comfort. It never portrays God's grace in Christ abstractly or as a matter merely to be committed to memory. It always portrays God's grace as engendering and shaping the Christian life.

In this the catechism, of course, simply follows the Scriptures: "As therefore you received Christ Jesus the Lord, so live in him" (Col. 2:6). Calvin put it nicely: "God the Father, as he has reconciled us to himself in his Christ, has in him stamped for us the likeness to which he would have us conform" (*Institutes* 3, vi, 3).

Jesus Christ is Lord. That reality continues to be central to the church's proclamation and central to the Christian life. All reflection about our personal lives and our life together properly begins by acknowledging that this Jesus, the anointed one, is Lord.

Jesus

Jesus means "savior." If we ask why he is called Jesus, the answer is simply, as the catechism says, "Because he saves us from our sins. Salvation cannot be found in anyone else; it is futile to look for any salvation elsewhere" (Q & A 29). That answer seems familiar enough, even tame enough. But it stops being tame as soon as we refuse to domesticate the reply by unduly and unbiblically restricting the meaning and scope of "savior" and "save" and "salvation." The biblical use of this vocabulary is broad and profound. The salvation celebrated and contemplated in the Bible has political and economic dimensions.

When Exodus 15:2, for example, sings of the Lord, "The Lord is my strength and my song, and he has become my salvation," it celebrates Israel's liberation from economic exploitation and political oppression in Egypt. When Isaiah sings of the Lord that he alone is Savior (Isa. 43:11, 45:21), the prophet contemplates a new state of affairs wrought by God's righteousness and strength; he contemplates the cosmic reign of God; he contemplates shalom (see, e.g., Isaiah 43:14–21; 45:22–25). And when Mary sings her wonderful Magnificat (Luke 1:46–55), she celebrates God's regard for her as the beginning of God's activity of raising the humble, humbling the exalted, feeding the hungry, and judging the rich. The salvation of God celebrated in Scripture may not be reduced to its political and economic dimensions, but it may not be emptied of them either.

If the vocabulary of the Scriptures does not convince us that God's salvation has political and economic dimensions, then looking at Jesus should. "Jesus" was a common enough name for a Jewish man. There may even have been more than one Jesus in Nazareth. But it was Mary's son who became notorious, got into trouble in Jerusalem with the authorities, and was put to death on a Roman cross for political insurrection; and it was Mary's son who is the Savior.

His name was Jesus, like my name is Allen. That's what his friends called him. His enemies called him lots of things (and he had lots of enemies). But "Jesus" was not a name Mary and Joseph chose because they liked the sound of it. An angel told Joseph the name; "You shall call his name Jesus," he said, "for he will save his people from their sins" (Matt. 1:21). And when an angel announced his birth to some simple shepherds, he said, "I bring you good news of a great joy which will come to all the people; for to you is born this day in the city of David a Savior, who is Christ the Lord" (Luke 2:10–11).

But perhaps the Christmas story, too, has become so familiar to us that it seems very comfortable and tame. If so, we should study it more carefully. Unto us was born a Savior, but that Savior came as a little, bawling child, born to humble, poor, simple peasants in a stable with the stench of manure. Perhaps it is pleasant enough—and tame enough—to think that divine life and divine purpose joined human life and human purposes, but that they joined at such a point is far from pleasant or tame. That Jesus, the Savior, enters human life where people are lowly rather than proud, where they are weak rather than strong, where they are poor and powerless is hardly "comforting" to people like me.

Mary was right. God's blessing upon her in the birth of Jesus was the beginning of God's decisive liberation of the poor and lowly and his judgment of the rich and proud. What was blessing to the humble Mary is judgment to people like me. Often I have intended good things for myself, heedless of the hungry. Often I have protected my interests and privileges, inattentive to the needy. Often I have been proud of the little good I do well, while the poor and powerless suffer and weep. Jesus, the Savior, born to the poor and humble and powerless, exposes my selfishness, complacency, and pretensions. "It is futile to look for any salvation elsewhere" (Q & A 29), even in a Jesus of my own comfortable and self-serving imagination. But the good news of the Christmas story, the good news of the catechism, is that this Jesus "saves us from our sins." My only comfort is that I belong to this Savior.

65

So, let the humble glory in that they are exalted; let Mary magnify the Lord. But let the rich and the powerful and the "good" people (like me) glory in that they are made low (James 1:9, 10). Mary's Magnificat becomes our song, too, when our spirits rejoice in God the Savior, for he has regarded the pride of his servants. He has done great things for us. He does not leave us in our bondage to wealth and pomp and privilege. By intending good things for the poor, he turns us from intending good things only for ourselves. By receiving the needy, he turns us from sending the needy away. By siding with the poor and powerless, he keeps us from turning to the rich and powerful.

He humbles the proud and exalts the humble, and thus has wrought his salvation. He is the Savior. There is none other—not money, not power, not fame. His name is Jesus, born to the poor and humble and powerless. Even so and only so is he born the Savior to us.

Acknowledging the reality of this Jesus as our Savior commits us to stand up for the rights of the poor, to side with the powerless, to visit the fatherless and widows, to deliver people from oppression, to protect people against exploitation. In such ways we live the catechism. His name is Jesus, Savior, Deliverer, Liberator, and he is and will be true to his name. Try as we may to make him false to his name by divorcing the salvation of souls from the salvation, the shalom, the new order, of God's righteousness, he is and will be true to his name. And we must be true to him, faithful to him, lest it be true of us that "although they boast of being his, by their deeds they deny the only savior and deliverer, Jesus" (Q & A 30).

Christ

This Jesus is the Christ, the "anointed." He is called Christ "because he has been ordained by God the Father and has been anointed with the Holy Spirit to be our chief prophet . . . , our only high priest . . . , and our eternal king . . ." (Q & A 31). Prophet, priest, and king, of course, are social roles; so, to confess with the catechism that Jesus is the Christ will certainly have social implications.

Jesus himself inaugurated his ministry with his claim to be anointed with the Spirit. "The Spirit of the Lord is upon me," he said, "because he has anointed me to preach good news to the poor. He has sent me to proclaim release to the captives and recovering of sight to the blind, to set at liberty those who are oppressed, to proclaim the acceptable year of the Lord" (Luke 4:18–19). Jesus is the Christ as the Savior, as the Liberator and Deliverer. He is the Christ, the anointed one, precisely because he has liberated the poor and oppressed. Expectations of the Christ are not removed from our world and our history and our social reality. That Jesus is the Christ, anointed to be prophet, priest, and king, is a social reality—and his righteousness as prophet, priest, and king is a social righteousness. We cannot acknowledge Jesus as the Christ without also acknowledging the gift and claims of a social reality and a social righteousness. We must live our confession.

"But why are you called a Christian?" the catechism asks. And its memorable reply makes it very clear that our confession that Jesus is the Christ must have an impact on our daily living: "Because by faith I am a member of Christ and so I share in his anointing. I am anointed to confess his name, to present myself to him as a living sacrifice of thanks, to strive with a good conscience against sin and the devil in this life, and afterward to reign with Christ over all creation for all eternity" (Q & A 32). The Spirit makes us "share in Christ and all his blessings" (Q & A 53)—and in his anointing.

That means we share in Christ and his righteousness, including his social righteousness. The grace of God in Christ, anointed to be prophet, priest, and king, engenders our real participation in those same offices. We are prophets, priests, and rulers and are called and obliged to fulfill the responsibilities of those offices. They are for us, as they were for the original prophets, priests, and kings—and as they were for the great prophet, priest, and king—social roles with social responsibilities.

Prophet

Jesus is the Christ, the anointed one, as prophet. The office of prophet gives us no license to abstract Jesus from our life amid social injustice and inequities. Prophets protested against injustice. They dissented from oppression. They condemned a social status quo that did not image God's righteousness. They irritated, embarrassed, and denounced the unjust rulers and the greedy merchants. They were the scourge of the smug and complacent. They uncovered and revealed corruption, whether at the scales of the marketplace or at the scales of justice. They did these things not alongside of, not in spite of, but precisely because of their calling to confess God's name. They saved their harshest words for those who named God's name without caring about justice, without feeding the hungry, without committing themselves to his covenant righteousness. It is no accident that prophets denounced social unrighteousness; they knew the righteousness of God.

Christ was *the* prophet anointed "to preach good news to the poor . . . to set at liberty those who are oppressed" (Luke 4:18). He judged the rich, the powerful, the complacent, the privileged. He blessed the poor, the hungry, the powerless (see, e.g. Luke 6:20–26). He revealed the "counsel and will of God for our deliverance" (Q & A 31)—and that surely included the prophetic conscience that demanded social righteousness.

We can have it no other way. We cannot pick and choose that part of deliverance we feel "comfortable" with. We cannot choose that part of God's counsel that doesn't disturb us or our status quo. We cannot opt for the sort of righteousness that doesn't demand much repentance or change. Christ, the anointed prophet, is and promises and demands our social righteousness.

And by our membership in Christ we are called to be prophets. We are called to discern and judge the injustice that keeps the poor from getting a hearing today, the inequity that keeps the hungry from getting fed today, the prejudice that oppresses Spanish Americans and blacks and women and the unborn today. As prophets, overwhelmed by the righteousness of God, we are called to model and demand that righteousness in our cities and villages and states and nations.

Prophets beat against ragged injustice with their bare hands. It hurts to be a prophet. But as such we are—all of us—called to confess his name, the "name which is above every name" (Phil. 2:9). And we're called to do that not just in the comfortable confines of like-minded people, but in the presence of those who accept or promote injustice in the social order and those who accept or promote a religious life that is comfortable with such injustice. Contemporary prophets will announce and believe and live that Jesus—not money, not power, not fame, not technology, not country, not suburbia—is Lord.

Being a prophet will demand our best and simplest gifts. We may find various ways to be prophets, but prophets we are—and must be.

Priest

Jesus is the Christ, the anointed one, also as priest. Surely he is not the sort of priest denounced by the prophets (e.g., Amos 5:21, 24: "I hate, I despise your feasts, and I take no delight in your solemn assemblies. . . . But let justice roll down like waters, and righteousness like an ever-flowing stream"). The true priest, of course, joined the prophet in this criticism of religion devoid of the fruits of righteousness. And Jesus, both as prophet and as priest, insisted on mercy rather than sacrifice, on reconciliation before leaving one's gift on the altar (Matt. 5:23–24, 12:7; Heb.10:5–7).

The epistle to the Hebrews helps us see the qualifications of Jesus as the one true high priest. He was made "like his brethren in every respect" (Heb. 2:17), even "tempted as we are" (4:15). By his full participation in human life and its temptation, he can "sympathize with our weaknesses" (4:15). Yet he met temptation "without sinning" and so he was qualified, "holy, blameless, [and] unstained," to provide himself as sacrifice for others (7:26–28). He "did not exalt himself to be made a high priest" (5:5); he humbled himself and took the form of a servant. He "learned obedience through what he suffered" (5:8). So he achieved the "perfection" that qualified him to act as the true and only high priest.

We do not do justice to the riches of the Christology of Hebrews or to the office of priest if we exclude moral perfection from the perfection achieved by Christ. Indeed, Hebrews puts one of the prophetic criticisms of a priesthood without fruits of obedience on the very lips of Jesus: "Sacrifices and offerings thou hast not desired. . . . 'Lo, I have come to do thy will, O God' " (Heb.10:5–7; citing Ps.40:6–8). So Jesus' obedience to the point of death is accepted as "for all time a single sacrifice for sins." And

God exalted him, set him at his right hand to await the complete subjection of his enemies (Heb. 10:12–13). We do not yet see all his enemies as a stool for his feet, but Jesus has won the victory. He is the perfect liberator, the "pioneer." He sets people free from real human bondage and makes his brothers and sisters "perfect" too (2:10 ff., 10:14).

That perfection includes moral perfection. It demands that we become involved in the real world in which we live. It demands that we continually struggle against the powers of evil, including the temptations in wealth to avarice and in power to tyranny. The perfection given by the true high priest makes us servants; we may not exalt ourselves. "Through him then let us continually offer up a sacrifice of praise to God, that is, the fruit of lips that acknowledge his name. Do not neglect to do good and to share what you have, for such sacrifices are pleasing to God" (Heb. 13:15, 16).

The only high priest calls for and consecrates our praise and our obedience. If we confess with the catechism that he is anointed high priest, then we commit ourselves to lives marked by the same obedience, the same suffering love. To live the catechism, to share in his anointing, we must do good and share what we have.

We have sometimes misunderstood the Protestant doctrine of "the priesthood of all believers." We have supposed that it means simply that each one can be his or her own priest. Such individualism, however, is far from the biblical talk about a royal priesthood (1 Pet. 2:9–10). In fact, the exact opposite is closer to the biblical understanding: everyone is a priest to every other one.

By our participation in Christ the priest, we are enabled and required to offer ourselves in patient love for others according to the pattern laid down by him. In Christ the priest, we present ourselves as living sacrifices (Q & A 32)—our bodies and our minds, our work and our leisure, our conversations with other people and our conversations about other people. We present our total life in praise and obedience. In Christ the priest, we find the courage to live in our costly comfort; sharing in his anointing means conforming to his patient love. So we do not neglect to do good and to share with those in need.

We must disavow any individualistic interpretation of our office of priest. The "priesthood of all believers" is the emphatic assertion of the privilege and obligation of each to serve the other—to pray for, encourage, support, admonish, love the other. The one high priest makes us a community of priests in and for the world.

Being priests will demand our best and simplest gifts. We may find diverse ways to be priests to each other and to the world, but priests we are—and must be.

King

Jesus is the Christ, the anointed one, finally, as king. No theme stirred the feelings of Israel more deeply than the theme "The Lord is

King." Many of the songs of Israel celebrate God's rule (Ps. 47, 93, 96–99). The enthusiasm and joy are nearly as large as God's realm. "Clap your hands, all peoples! Shout to God with loud songs of joy" (Ps. 47:1). Why? Because "God is the king of all the earth" (Ps. 47:7). All nature and all history have their destiny under this king, and all are invited to join in his praise. And he is worthy of praise, for he is a "lover of justice" (Ps. 99:4). "He will judge the world with righteousness, and the peoples with equity" (Ps. 98:9).

Such celebrations of God's rule are not left to one side in the consideration of temporal kingship. The earthly king of David's line is the anointed, the chosen servant, the representative of God. Psalm 72 lists the qualities of a king worthy of his anointment. The temporal king, too, is to be a lover of justice. "Give the king thy justice, O God, and thy righteousness to the royal son! May he judge thy people with righteousness and thy poor with justice! Let the mountains bear prosperity for the people, and the hills, in righteousness! May he defend the cause of the poor of the people, give deliverance to the needy, and crush the oppressor!" (Ps. 72:1–4).

Such portrayals of kings stand in critical and creative tension with the kings themselves, of course. The prophets bore witness to that tension. The righteous king in the portrayal is humble. He does not exalt himself. He uses his power not for himself or his own aggrandizement but to defend the powerless. His prestige and honor are not in pomp and protocol but in his compassion and service. His sign of royalty is his humility.

So the Christ, the anointed king, comes mounted on a colt. Here is the humble king; here is the righteousness of God; here is justice, equity, peace; here is deliverance for the poor, liberation for the oppressed; here is the king of kings; here is our social righteousness.

And we are members of Christ the king. We share in his anointing as king. We easily stumble here. We are too filled with our own ideas of ruling. So were the disciples. The mother of the sons of Zebedee wanted Jesus to put her sons at his right and left hand in the kingdom. Jesus answered, "You do not know what you are asking. Are you able to drink the cup that I am to drink?" (Matt. 20:22). There is no place for pride here, no place for the "arrogance of power," no place for status-seeking or power-grabbing. To participate in Christ the king is to be a humble servant, to drink the cup of his passion. Where Christ is king, service is the mark of royalty.

Triumphalism has no place here either. The catechism makes it clear that to participate in Christ the king means now that we "strive with a good conscience against sin and the devil in this life" (Q & A 32). Of course, the catechism knows that the decisive battle has been fought and won. Christ is king. He sits at his Father's right hand in power. But it also knows that that great victory is not yet complete.

The catechism drafts us now against the powers of evil in all of life; whoever confesses the catechism enlists in a struggle that is also social.

Oppression, injustice, corruption, and prejudice have not yet laid down their arms and admitted defeat. Here and now, in the interim between the decisive victory and the final one, we will face skirmishes. To participate in Christ the king is to be a dutiful soldier, contending against the principalities, powers, world rulers (cf. Eph. 6:11, referred to by Q & A 32).

The skirmishes in which Christians strive for their king against sin and the devil take place on many different fronts. We may not forget that the whole cosmos fell under the usurpation of sin or that Christ says, "Behold, I make all things new" (Rev. 21:5). On the environmental front our participation in Christ the king makes us militant against pollution. On the economic front we strive against exploitation and inequity. In race relations we contend against prejudice and discrimination. In every area of our life we are called to "strive . . . against sin and the devil."

Those who confess the catechism begin to see all power as an opportunity for service. Political power, including the powers to vote and dissent and express, is held not as "the rulers of the Gentiles [who] lord it over them" (Matt. 20:25), but as an opportunity to image Christ the king, who took the form of a servant. Economic power, including the powers to buy and sell and lend and borrow and hire and fire, is seen in light of the same law of service under the same humble king who maintains the cause of the needy and blesses the poor. The cross is lifted over us; we journey— even politically, economically, racially—in its light. The crown awaits the conquest—the day when Christ the king will say to those who have given food to the hungry and drink to the thirsty, " 'Come, O blessed of my Father, inherit the kingdom prepared for you' " (Matt. 25:34, referred to by Q & A 32).

Being rulers will demand our best and simplest gifts. We may find diverse ways to be servant rulers, but rulers we are—and servant rulers in the midst of the world we must be.

Lord

And this Jesus, anointed to be prophet, priest, and king, is Lord. That is decisive. "If you confess with your lips that Jesus is Lord and believe in your heart that God raised him from the dead, you will be saved" (Rom. 10:9). The catechism here reiterates the theme of its comfort—that we are not our own but belong, body and soul, to our faithful savior Jesus Christ. "Why do you call him our Lord? Because— not with gold or silver, but with his precious blood—he has set us free from sin and from the tyranny of the devil, and has bought us, body and soul, to be his very own" (Q & A 34). Our only comfort is the reality that Jesus Christ is Lord. That costly comfort, that reality, is the point of departure for our social reflection and action.

The early church, under the constraint of this simple but profound confession, put the Roman government to shame by providing food for the hungry and shelter for the homeless. Under the obligation of that confession, Christians put an end to the slaughtering spectacle of gladiator contests and to the abandonment of infants. With that confession Paul had the courage to confront Governor Felix. Felix had asked about Jesus Christ, thinking perhaps to gain some relief from the pressures of administration, some easy comfort for a troubled conscience. But Paul responded with talk about justice and self-control and the future judgment (Acts 24:25). Paul talked about Jesus Christ all right. He proclaimed him as the one who disarmed the principalities and powers, the one who triumphed over them in his cross and resurrection. He proclaimed him as Lord and as our social righteousness. And Felix was alarmed, for Felix found this reality threatening.

Felix learned that whatever else the Lord's comfort is, it is not cheap. It cannot be bought. It cannot be used. It can only be received as gift and as demand. The costly comfort is not that the Lord is ours but that, body and soul, socially and personally, politically and privately, we are the Lord's. No one and no thing may usurp his throne. We may not say "Jesus Christ is Lord, but so is Caesar"—for Jesus is also the Lord of our citizenship. We may not say "Jesus Christ is Lord, but so is mammon"—for Jesus is Lord of our money. We cannot say "Jesus Christ is Lord, but so is white, middle-class Protestantism"—for Jesus is Lord of our religion. The confession that Jesus is Lord leaves no little corner of our life or our society's life an empire of its own.

Jesus' crucifixion and resurrection were long ago. He won the victory in a time and culture very different from our own. But the lordship of this liberator, this true prophet, priest, and king, is very contemporary. And the call for justice that goes out from the righteousness of God is equally contemporary. Jesus Christ is Lord now. He sits now at God's right hand. Injustice rules in our society, and vanity mars our religious life. Our ambiguous historical reality does not yet conform to the reality of Christ's resurrection and lordship. But the comfort of the gospel continues to be the confession that Jesus Christ is Lord.

Those who hold to the catechism commit themselves to make that confession not only with their lips but also with their lives, not only in the comfortable confines of like-minded people but also in the threatening company of those who promote injustice or accept complacency. The catechism is no easy confession. Felix told Paul to leave, and many of us might protect our honesty by telling the Heidelberger to leave. To say and mean that Jesus Christ is Lord is probably the most threatening thing that anyone can do. But that is what the catechism asks of us.

The church cannot say Jesus Christ is Lord and then be complacent about the injustice that remains in society. Nor can we say Jesus Christ is Lord and then be ungrateful to God for those whose lives have promoted justice. The church must say he is Lord not just on Easter or Ascension Day but on Independence Day and Memorial Day and Labor Day, on Election Day and today. It is not easy, but he has freed us and bought us to be his very own. It is not easy, but it is possible in the victory of his resurrection and in the freedom of the truth.

Liberation

Jesus Christ is Lord. That reality remains central to the church's proclamation and to the Christian life. Because that confession is also a social reality, the church's proclamation and the Christian life will and must include social and political and economic dimensions. When and if the church no longer announces and reflects and serves this reality, then the church is no longer true or faithful. The church may still "boast of being his," but it is by our deeds, according to the catechism, that we will finally affirm or deny that Jesus Christ is Lord (Q & A 30).

There is, as Howard Hageman says, a "great ethical thrust" in the catechism. "Where its point of view is taken seriously," he says,

> there can be no passive acceptance of whatever takes place in government or in the social order as "none of the church's business." What would the man from Heidelberg make out of the common assertion of the *soi-disant* orthodox Reformed of today that the "church should stick to preaching the gospel and saving souls"? If I read the catechism correctly, it would answer that we have not really preached the gospel unless the souls that have been saved have been sent out into the world with a tremendous passion to bring the total pattern of the world's existence under obedience to the kingdom of Christ.

It will always remain, therefore, the responsibility of churches that confess the catechism to think about and talk about and pray about the specific social policies and concrete political actions that most befit the lordship of Jesus Christ. And it is in the churches, not on these pages, that the lordship of Jesus Christ takes concrete (if imperfect) form. The attempt here is to make a small contribution to the thought and talk and prayers and life of churches who are trying to live as well as recite the catechism.

The lordship of Jesus Christ lays claim to our whole life and to every part of it. Here I propose to focus on what it might mean to live the catechism in a world where liberation movements of one kind or another abound.

We may begin with the affirmation that this Jesus, this "perfect savior," this complete liberator, is Lord. There is no ignoring the catechism's interest in "liberation." The Lord Jesus Christ "was given us to set us completely free" (Q & A 18). As our king, he "guards us and keeps us in the freedom he has won for us" (Q & A 31). The catechism's treatment, moreover, of the Christian confession that Jesus Christ is Lord does not entitle us to restrict the liberation he has won to a narrow "private" or "cultic" or "inner" sphere. We are not entitled to think that the Savior has no relation to the "liberation movements" of our world—black liberation, gray liberation, women's liberation, Third-World liberation, gay liberation, and so forth. But what is the relation?

73

The catechism holds us, I suggest, to a dialectical relationship to such movements, to a relationship at once supportive and critical. On the one hand, we know that we cannot grasp faith while we refuse the obligation to work bodily and politically to liberate people from real oppression, real injustice, and real affliction. We know—or ought to know—that the proclamation "Jesus Christ is Lord," the good news that this Jesus was born to the poor and powerless, that he was anointed to be prophet, priest, and king, and that he was lifted up to all authority is not an "opium of the people." It is not something that incapacitates and enervates, but rather a leaven of freedom and justice. So we speak an unequivocal "no" to the bondage under which women and blacks and Third-World peoples and others are held and an impassioned "yes" to their struggles for liberation.

But, on the other hand, we know that complete liberation is found only in Christ Jesus (Q & A 30), and we are ready to be critical of such liberation movements when and if they become idolatrous or nurture enmity and self-righteousness. They become idolatrous when all human values are judged relative to the interests of the group they seek to free, when the cause becomes the only and final measure of worth, when the genuine but partial justice they seek is made the absolute and total human good. For example, the black liberation movement is sometimes tempted to say that whatever serves the black cause is good, whatever doesn't is evil. And the women's liberation movement is sometimes tempted to say that if something serves the interests of women—removing legal restrictions on abortion, for instance—then it is good.

Such absolute and pretentious claims for the interests of any one group can nurture self-righteousness and enmity. Liberation movements are sometimes tempted to identify and then to hate "the enemy," the one who stands in the way of the cause—whether that be the white race, males, developed countries, or some other group. Those who own the catechism as a standard must say "no" to both pride and hatred. Whenever liberation movements become idolatrous, those who own the catechism must say to them, "No, not where Christ is Lord."

Liberation movements that are idolatrous or nurture enmity and self-righteousness will never achieve genuine liberation. At best they may bring about an exchange of roles between the oppressor and the oppressed and at worst subjection to a new form of bondage. The church's task of liberation necessarily involves her in a battle against the principalities and powers that hold people in bondage, sometimes including liberation movements. The church must be ready to respond critically as well as supportively to the liberation movements in our world.

The readiness to respond both supportively and critically demands that we listen to attentively and try to understand sympathetically the many cries for liberation in our world. That we often fail to do even that is due to our tendency to respond defensively. But the defensive posture has no place where Jesus Christ is Lord, where it is Jesus and not any privileged position which is our only comfort, our faithful Savior. Jesus can be trusted; privilege needs not be defended and protected. Before we can respond to liberation movements faithfully, then—before we can criticize them responsibly—we must cry out for our own liberation, for a liberation movement among the privileged.

A liberation movement among the privileged would deal with racism, for white Christians can never be truly or completely free as long as they deny the equal humanity of others. White Christians will have to think and talk and pray not only about their personal intentions and dispositions but also about their complacency with social structures that effectively preserve their privileges and deny equal benefit or equal opportunity to blacks and other ethnic minorities. White Christians must begin to cry out for liberation from their own bondage to this evil power of racism that binds them both personally and institutionally.

A liberation movement among the privileged would deal with • sexism, for male Christians cannot be truly or completely free as long as they use or denigrate women. Male Christians need to think about and talk about and pray about the stereotypes and role assignments and sexual humor and sexual harrassment that oppress women and sustain inequities and injustices in society—not only for the sake of the liberation of women but also for the liberation of men. Male Christians must begin to cry out for liberation from their own bondage to this evil power of sexism that binds them both personally and structurally. Males may thus be freed to be more nurturing fathers, more compassionate friends, more able to shed a tear at another's sadness or to share an embrace in celebration of another's being.

A liberation movement among the privileged would deal with ageism, with the nationalism of First World nations, and with much besides. But in all of it power would be a central issue. In most liberation movements power is essential to liberation, but the privileged already have power. What they need for true and complete liberation is a new way of seeing and using that power. Jesus provided that new way; he said, "You know that those who are supposed to rule over the Gentiles lord it over them, and their great men exercise authority over them. But it shall not be so among you; but whoever would be great among you must be your servant, and whoever would be first among you must be slave of all. For the Son of man also came not to be served but to serve, and to give his life as a ransom for many" (Mark 10:42–45).

The perfect Savior frees us from that "Gentile" notion of power. He does not free us from power itself. He does not make us powerless. To disown power and the use of power, as though it had been replaced by or equated with love, is to fantasize about our world. But Jesus does free us to see power as an opportunity to serve and empower rather than to "lord it over them." He does liberate us to be stewards of our power, to use it for the good of our neighbor.

The liberation of the rich is not new, of course. Jesus, born to the poor and humble and powerless, liberated the privileged during his lifetime. Many resisted their own liberation, of course—like the rich man of

Mark 10:17–22. But Zacchaeus, a rich and powerful tax collector, received Jesus joyfully (Luke 19:1–10). He did justice (restoring four times what he had gained by cheating) and practiced charity (giving half his goods to the poor), and Jesus said to him, "Today salvation has come to this house" (v. 9).

The church that follows Jesus and confesses that he is and will be true to his name is called to the task of liberation and enlisted in the struggle against the principalities and powers that hold people, including ourselves, in bondage. In Ephesians 3:10 Paul prays "that through the church the manifold wisdom of God might now be made known to the principalities and powers in the heavenly places." The very existence of the church should be a sign of liberation. Here Jew and Gentile are freed from the pride and enmity that divided them. They are freed to live together in Christ's fellowship.

To be such a community is one task, the first and fundamental task, that Christ the liberator-Lord gives the church. The church must be a community that bears the fruit of a "perfect Savior" and bears the promise of his cosmic reign, a community where "there is neither Jew nor Greek, there is neither slave nor free, there is neither male nor female" (Gal. 3:28).

Of course, Paul did not lead any slave revolt—or even call for one. But his advice to both slaves and masters recognized one Master before whom they were both equal and in whom they were one (e.g., Eph. 6:5–9). The institution of slavery could not endure the leaven of freedom in the proclamation that Jesus Christ is Lord. We no longer question whether the abolitionists or the defenders of slavery were using the Bible correctly. In faithful response to Jesus the liberator, slavery finally had to go.

It is no different with the equality and unity of men and women in Jesus Christ the Lord. Again, Paul did not lead or call for "a woman's year," but he did announce that Jesus is Lord. And while certain passages can be chosen to support institutional inequities (as with slavery), the leaven of freedom in the gospel and in the catechism calls us to put stereotypes and inequities behind us and to put on the unity and equality of men and women in Christ. Where the one who would be great must be a servant, women may not seek equality without a willingness to be ministers. And where authority means serving and empowering, men may not pick and choose the kinds of leadership and, therefore, service open to women.

It is not insignificant that the word used in the New Testament to refer to ministry, to authority in the church, is *diakonia*, which meant originally "to wait at table, serving food and pouring wine and cleaning up." While the word came to have the more general meaning of providing for and caring for, it never quite lost its flavor of inferiority. It was, quite frankly, not quite proper for a man, at least a free man, to be a *diakonos*, a minister. If ministry in the church means the sort of service women render, then it is curious that anyone should think women unfit for leadership in the church.

The church still confesses that Jesus is the liberator, the Savior. To live that confession is to be a community in which genuine liberation occurs, where men do not "lord it over" women, where men and women serve and empower one another in and for ministry. The subjugation of women will not finally be able to tolerate the leaven of freedom in the proclamation that Jesus Christ is Lord.

The leaven of liberation is given to the church in Jesus the Savior. The unity and equality of its members are given to the church in Christ the Lord. But the gift is also a claim, a calling; and it comes to the church today not only as gift and as calling but as judgment. As a sociological entity the church stands exposed, accepting and reflecting the divisions and inequities of the world. The empirical church has sometimes bent its knee before the principalities and powers, before nationalism, racism, sexism, mammon, privilege, and the rest. But, by God's mercies, the leaven of liberation and of the unity and equality in Christ comes today not only as claim and as judgment but also as comfort and courage and grace and power.

Jesus Christ the Lord still sits at the right hand of God, far above every principality and power and might and dominion and every name that is named, and he is still "given us to set us completely free" (Q & A 18). From this gift the church has the power to be his body—a community that images his righteousness, a community where genuine liberation occurs, where the unity and equality in Christ consistently and constantly challenge both old and new forms of pride, enmity, and inequity. From this gift the church has the courage to minister in and for the world, to be a leaven of liberation in and for the world, to wrestle against the powers that divide people, that break solidarity and create pretensions of inequality, and that cause love to miscarry.

So the church will be ready to listen attentively and sympathetically to voices raised in cries for liberation and ready to respond, not defensively, but supportively and critically. We may not be inattentive to either persons or social structures (including ecclesiastical structures) when we live the catechism's confession that Jesus Christ is Lord. "As therefore you received Christ Jesus the Lord, so live in him" (Col. 2:6).

Acknowledgments and Suggestions for Further Reading

The quotation of Howard Hageman is from his essay "The Catechism in Christian Nurture," Bard Thomson et al., *Essays on the Heidelberg Catechism* (Philadelphia: United Church Press, 1963), pp. 173–174.

The literature on the theme of liberation is enormous. J. Verkuyl's *The Message of Liberation in Our Age*, translated by Dale Cooper (Grand Rapids: Wm. B. Eerdmans, 1970), provides a readable and general introduction. Gustavo Gutierrez's *A Theology of Liberation* (London: SCM Press, 1974) is written from the perspective of a Latin American Christian. James

Cone's *A Black Theology of Liberation* (Philadelphia: Lippincott, 1970) is written from the perspective of an American black Christian. Rosemary Ruether's *Liberation Theology* (New York: Paulist Press, 1970) is a general account, but written from the perspective of a woman.

Dr. Martin Luther King, Jr.'s "Letter from a Birmingham Jail," cited in the questions for discussion, can be found in Henry Steele Commager, ed., *The Struggle for Racial Equality: A Documentary Record* (New York: Harper & Row, 1967), pp. 145–162. I would highly recommend the book of Allan Boesak, *Farewell to Innocence* (Maryknoll, N.Y.: Orbis Books, 1977).

Discussion Questions for Chapter 6

1. It's 1830, and the slavery controversy is shaking the nation and disrupting the churches. Some church leaders are calling for "immediate emancipation" and "liberation." Others depict such abolitionists as liberals who reject the Word of God; they are quick to quote Ephesians 6:5 and to say (as Benjamin Morgan, of the First Presbyterian Church of New Orleans, said), "We defend the cause of God." The controversy finds its way to your congregation. Which side do you take? Why? What about the Word of God? What is the cause of God?

2. Now it's April 16, 1963. Martin Luther King, Jr. sits in a Birmingham jail after defying an injunction against demonstrations against segregation. Eight white clergymen denounce him publicly as an "outside agitator." Dr. King responds with his memorable "Letter from a Birmingham Jail":

> I am in Birmingham because injustice is here. Just as the prophets of the eighth century B.C. left their villages and carried their "thus saith the Lord" far beyond the boundaries of their hometowns, . . . so I am compelled to carry the gospel of freedom beyond my own hometown. . . .
>
> In the midst of blatant injustices inflicted upon the Negro, I have watched white churchmen stand on the sideline and mouth pious irrelevancies and sanctimonious trivialities. In the midst of a mighty struggle to rid our nation of racial and economic injustice, I have heard many ministers say, "Those are social issues, with which the gospel has no real concern. . . ."
>
> In deep disappointment I have wept over the laxity of the church. But be assured that my tears have been tears of love. There can be no deep disappointment where there is not deep love. Yes, I see the church as the body of Christ. But, oh! How we have blemished and scarred that body through social neglect and through fear of being nonconformists.

This controversy finds its way into your congregation, too. Do you agree with Dr. King or his detractors? Why? How do the catechism's treatment of the prophetic office of believers, the liberation Christ gives and demands, and the social reality of Jesus Christ as Lord bear on Dr. King's letter?

There were one hundred years between the Emancipation Proclamation and Dr. King's letter. Is the struggle for black liberation accomplished yet? Explain.

3. It's today. The controversy about the ordination of women is disrupting the churches. Some leaders of the church are calling for immediate freedom to ordain women. Others depict such leaders as liberals who reject the Word of God. Which side do you take? Why? How do your reasons compare with what you said in response to question 1? What is the cause of God? What about the Word of God? If the cause and Word are different, what justifies the difference?

7

MEMBERSHIP IN CHRIST

Q. What further advantage do we receive
   from Christ's sacrifice and death on the cross?

A. Through Christ's death
   our old selves are crucified, put to death, and buried with him,
   so that the evil desires of the flesh
      may no longer rule us,
   but that instead we may dedicate ourselves
      as an offering of gratitude to him.
                        —Heidelberg Catechism Q & A 43

Q. How does Christ's resurrection
   benefit us?

A. First, by his resurrection he has overcome death,
      so that he might make us share in the righteousness
      he won for us by his death.

   Second, by his power we too
      are already now resurrected to a new life.

   Third, Christ's resurrection
      is a guarantee of our glorious resurrection.
                        —Heidelberg Catechism Q & A 45

Q. What do you believe
   concerning "The Holy Spirit"?

A. *First, he, as well as the Father and the Son,*
   is eternal God.

   Second, he has been given to me personally,
   so that, by true faith,
   he makes me share in Christ and all his blessings,
   comforts me,
   and remains with me forever.
                                    —*Heidelberg Catechism Q & A 53*

Q. *What do you believe*
   concerning the "holy catholic church"?

A. *I believe that the Son of God,*
   through his Spirit and Word,
   out of the entire human race,
   from the beginning of the world to its end,
   gathers, protects, and preserves for himself
   a community chosen for eternal life
   and united in true faith.
   And of this community I am and always will be
   a living member.
                                    —*Heidelberg Catechism Q & A 54*

Q. *What do you understand by*
   "the communion of saints"?

A. *First, that believers one and all,*
   as members of this community,
   share in Christ
   and in all his treasures and gifts.

   Second, that each member
   should consider it his duty
   to use his gifts
   readily and cheerfully
   for the service and enrichment
   of the other members.
                                    —*Heidelberg Catechism Q & A 55*

Q. *Why do you say that*
   by faith alone
   you are right with God?

A. *It is not because of any value my faith has*
   that God is pleased with me.
   Only Christ's satisfaction, righteousness, and holiness
   make me right with God.

And I can receive this righteousness and make it mine
  in no other way than
  by faith alone.

—Heidelberg Catechism Q & A 61

Q. But doesn't this teaching
  make people indifferent and wicked?

A. No.
  It is impossible
    for those grafted into Christ by true faith
  not to produce fruits of gratitude.

—Heidelberg Catechism Q & A 64

The death he died he died to sin, once for all, but the life he lives he lives to God. So you also must consider yourselves dead to sin and alive to God in Christ Jesus.

—Romans 6:10–11

I have been crucified with Christ; it is no longer I who live, but Christ who lives in me; and the life I now live in the flesh I live by faith in the Son of God, who loved me and gave himself for me.

—Galatians 2:20

But God, who is rich in mercy, out of the great love with which he loved us, even when we were dead through our trespasses, made us alive together with Christ (by grace you have been saved), and raised us up with him, and made us sit with him in the heavenly places in Christ Jesus, that in the coming ages he might show the immeasurable riches of his grace in kindness toward us in Christ Jesus. For by grace you have been saved through faith; and this is not your own doing, it is the gift of God—not because of works, lest any man should boast. For we are his workmanship, created in Christ Jesus for good works, which God prepared beforehand, that we should walk in them.

—Ephesians 2:4–10

He who says he abides in him ought to walk in the same way in which he walked.

—1 John 2:6

All that he possesses is nothing until we grow into one body with him.

—John Calvin, Institutes, *3, i, 1*

Being "in Christ" means being part of a program as broad as the universe. The new creation is not merely the renewal of individuals, though this must be given its due. . . . The design of Christ's new creation is far too grand, too inclusive to be restricted to what happens inside my soul. No nook or cranny of

83

history is too small, no cultural potential is too large for its embrace. Being in Christ, we are part of a new movement by his grace, a movement rolling on toward the new heaven and the new earth where all things are made right and where He is all in all.

—*Lewis Smedes,* Union with Christ

WE ARE CALLED CHRISTIANS because by faith we are members of Christ (Q & A 32). We share in Christ; we are united to Christ. In its stress on union with Christ, the catechism simply follows Paul, of course, and John Calvin. And, like Paul and Calvin, the catechism doesn't treat our union with Christ as "mystical union," the loss of self in the divinity of Christ. It treats it, rather, as an active union, as the conformity of our lives to the work of Christ.

The mystics stress participation in Christ's *being*, sometimes to the point of insisting that a person becomes Christ or is deified. Paul and Calvin and the catechism stress participation in Christ's *work*, in his acts, to the point of insisting that a person is called to conform to Christ's suffering, his death, his resurrection, and his reign.

The catechism has little sympathy for the mystical handling of union with Christ. We do not become Christ, says the Heidelberg. "Christ alone is the eternal, natural Son of God. We, however, are adopted children of God—adopted by grace through Christ" (Q & A 33). The *being* of Christ and the *being* of the believer remain quite distinct. The unity of Christ and the believer is, for the catechism, where the action is, where the great acts of God in Jesus Christ and his Spirit form and inform our lives until we conform to his righteousness—all of it. It is as Calvin said in the opening words of "the golden booklet on the Christian life" (*Institutes*, 3, vi-x), "The object of regeneration . . . is to manifest in the life of believers a harmony and agreement between God's righteousness and their obedience, and thus to confirm the adoption that they have received as sons" (3, vi, 1).

As we saw in the previous chapter, the catechism spells out our active union with Christ in terms of our participation in the social roles of prophet, priest, and ruler. As the catechism continues with the Apostles' Creed to recite the great acts of God in Jesus Christ and in his Spirit, it also continues to emphasize our membership in Christ, our participation in his work, our conformation to his righteousness, our active union with our Lord.

Sharing in His Cross and Resurrection

With the Apostles' Creed the catechism says that Jesus Christ, our Lord, "was conceived by the Holy Spirit, born of the virgin Mary; suffered under Pontius Pilate; was crucified, dead, and buried; he descended into hell; the third day he rose again from the dead; he ascended into heaven, and sitteth at the right hand of God the Father almighty; from thence he shall come to judge the living and the dead." The catechism's interest in these articles is a practical interest. The treatment is doctrinal, to be sure, but according to the catechism, as we have said again and again, doctrine must pass into life.

So the interest remains practical, and the inferences remain moral. The catechism never turns its back on life in this world. It consistently asks about the benefits of Christ's work to believers, and these benefits consistently call our attention to our duties as well as to God's grace. God's gracious action, after all, engenders and shapes our action, forms and informs lives of gratitude. Christ "was crucified, dead, and buried." And the "advantage," the "costly comfort," is that "through Christ's death our old selves are crucified, put to death, and buried with him, so that the evil desires of the flesh may no longer rule us, but that instead we may dedicate ourselves as an offering of gratitude to him" (Q & A 43). But God raised him up! And the "benefit," the "costly comfort," is "that he might make us share in the righteousness he won for us by his death. . . . By his power we too are already now resurrected to a new life" (Q & A 45).

The blessings of membership in Christ, then—the benefits, the advantages—are lives of gratitude and righteousness. The catechism does not add a section on the Christian life merely as a kind of appendix to the blessings of sharing in Christ. The costly comfort of sharing in Christ's righteousness is what the Christian life is all about. The beginning of the section on the Christian life reiterates and reemphasizes these costly blessings, this participation in the cross and resurrection of Christ. There it asks, "What is involved in genuine repentance or conversion?" And it answers, "The dying-away of the old self, and the coming-to-life of the new" (Q & A 88).

We miss the point if we take repentance and conversion to be simply first steps in the path of *ordo salutis*. Like Calvin, the catechism teaches that repentance and conversion are a continual part of the life of sanctification. Dying with Christ, the Heidelberg teaches, "is to be genuinely sorry for sin, to hate it more and more, and to run away from it" (Q & A 89). Being raised already with Christ "is wholehearted joy in God through Christ and a delight to do every kind of good as God wants us to" (Q & A 90).

This, then, is the foundation of the Christian life in the catechism: we share in the cross and resurrection of Christ. The catechism simply follows the Scripture here, of course. Romans 6:5–11, the passage used to confirm Questions and Answers 43, 45, 88, and 90, insists that we conform to that by which we are formed a new people. "The death he died he died to sin, once for all, but the life he lives he lives to God. So you also must consider yourselves dead to sin and alive to God in Christ Jesus" (Rom. 6:10, 11). On that basis Paul exhorts the Roman church to "yield yourselves to God as men who have been brought from death to life, and your members to God as instruments of righteousness" (Rom. 6:13).

"Instruments of righteousness" are tools of justice. The social implications of our participation in Christ should not be overlooked or neglected, as though being "in Christ" were, either for the New Testament or for the catechism, a non-social reality, an individual matter, or a mystical experience. Our participation in Christ is the foundation of a substantial (and costly) social posture. Sharing in Christ's death is "to be genuinely sorry for [racism], to hate [exploitation] more and more, and to run away from [injustice]". Sharing in Christ's resurrection is to "delight to do every kind of good [including social, political, and economic good] as God wants us to."

If we say that we abide in him, then we must walk in newness of life, the path of service, the way of righteousness. That service is not merely social righteousness, but it surely includes social righteousness. We may never renege on the social implications of the costly comfort that we belong totally to the crucified and risen Lord. To "dedicate ourselves as an offering of gratitude to him" (Q & A 43), to "share in his righteousness" (Q & A 45), to yield ourselves to God as "instruments of righteousness" (Rom. 6:13) includes being tools of justice.

A poem of Carl Sandburg puts it memorably:

Lay me on an anvil, O God.
Beat me and hammer me into a crowbar.
Let me pry loose old walls.
Let me lift and loosen old foundations.

Lay me on an anvil, O God.
Beat me and hammer me into a steel spike.
Drive me into the girders that hold a skyscraper together.
Take red-hot rivets and fasten me into the central girders.
Let me be the great nail holding a skyscraper through blue nights
    into white stars.

That poem expresses powerfully the Christian prayer that God make us new and that he make us his tools—his crowbars and spikes—to bring that same newness to our neighbors and to our society. We cannot pray to be made new without also praying to be made tools of his justice. Such prayers, such tools, such social intentions are formed by the engendering deed of Christ's cross and resurrection.

It is little wonder, then, that the catechism is so confident against the charge that its teaching makes people indifferent and wicked. "It is impossible," the catechism says, "for those grafted into Christ by true faith not to produce fruits of gratitude" (Q & A 64). God's act in Christ engenders and shapes our actions. Our union with Christ is an active union. It is finally "a doctrine not of the tongue but of life" (Calvin, *Institutes*, 3, vi, 4)

Do our lives—every part of them—proclaim the doctrine as clearly and as eagerly as our tongues do? Has the charge that the catechism's doctrine makes people indifferent and wicked been strengthened, or has the catechism's confidence against the charge been vindicated by our working and selling and buying; by our treatment of prisoners, outcasts, minorities, women; by our politicking, by our leading and our following, and by our care for the poor and hungry? Those are not comforting questions, but they are unavoidable for those who hold dear the catechism's comfort.

The Spirit and the Church

The Apostles' Creed continues: "I believe in the Holy Spirit; I believe a holy catholic church, the communion of saints; the forgiveness of sins; the resurrection of the body; and the life everlasting."

Through the Spirit we "share in Christ and all his blessings" (Q & A 53). These blessings, it may be said again, are lives of gratitude and righteousness, "our sanctification" (Q & A 24). Life in the Spirit is not some otherworldly or mystical experience; it is real life, this life, lived under the lordship of Jesus Christ and in conformity to his righteousness. So it was announced in the opening question: "Because I belong to him, Christ, by his Holy Spirit, assures me of eternal life and makes me whole-heartedly willing and ready from now on to live for him" (Q & A 1).

The ascended Lord gives us the Spirit as a "guarantee" (Q & A 49; 2 Cor. 1:22, 5:5; Eph. 1:14). The Spirit is the pledge, the earnest, the down payment on the future, the guarantee of the cosmic rule of Jesus Christ. The Spirit brings into our lives nothing other than the reality of Jesus Christ and his lordship and promises us nothing less than the new heaven and new earth of his reign. So the Spirit is an agent of renewal (Qs & As 8, 70, 86). "By the Spirit's power we make the goal of our lives, not earthly things, but the things above where Christ is, sitting at God's right hand" (Q & A 49). By the Spirit's power we intend—in all of our living—to recognize Christ's reign over all things. The promise of the Spirit is always precisely the promise of Christ: "Behold, I make all things new" (Rev. 21:5).

So much around us is broken—broken homes, broken promises of food and shelter, broken dreams of freedom and equity—that it sometimes seems that to believe this promise of newness is more sentimental than perceptive, more like wishful thinking than genuine Christian hope. We used to talk about this hemisphere as "the new world" and about ourselves as a new people. It was a great new experiment, and it was America, some said, that would usher in a prosperous and happy future for the world. But racial tensions, a horrible war, assassinations, and scandals have convinced us that such an understanding of ourselves is at best naive and probably presumptuous.

We cannot deny the brokenness of our world or of our political and social institutions. But the catechism assures us—in the midst of what is broken and spoiled by sin, in the midst of injustice and poverty and oppression—that Jesus Christ reigns and will reign and that the Spirit is the agent of his renewal.

"Behold, I make all things new." The words are "trustworthy and true" (Rev. 21:5). That's why the risen and ascended Lord told John to write them down. He makes things new by his Spirit. The Spirit was there at creation, brooding upon the waters of chaos and bringing to birth a new creation. The Spirit was there at that greater birth, bringing into being a new creature, Jesus of Nazareth; and in his ministry, anointing him with the power to be a new prophet, a new priest, and a new king; and in his grave, making new what was broken and dead, giving life where there was none. His Spirit was there at Pentecost, coming to the disciples like fire and like wind so that the power in others' lives was a new power, God's power. And his Spirit is at work today—brooding over the waters formed by the tears of the hungry and oppressed, brooding over the injustice and chaos of our lives together. The promise of the Spirit remains precisely the promise of Christ: "Behold, I make all things new."

The Spirit "has been given to me personally" (Q & A 53)—but not individualistically. When the Spirit gives unity with Christ, the Spirit gives community in the church. Our union with Christ through the Spirit makes us part of a communion. The Lord "gathers, protects, and preserves for himself a community chosen for eternal life and united in true faith" (Q & A 54). The catechism does not say, it is important to note, that he gathers, protects, and preserves individuals who are later and independently made members of the church. The Lord works out his purpose in a community, and it is in terms of this community that the individual introduced in the last phrase of Q & A 54 eloquently expresses his confidence: "of this community I am and always will be a living member."

Such confidence is not introspective, but social; it is the assurance of 1 John 3:14, "We know that we have passed out of death into life, because we love the brethren." It is important to call attention to the inclusiveness of this community in the catechism. We find nothing here about church growth along socially homogeneous lines, nothing about ethnic unity. Rather, the catechism confesses that Christ gathers this community "out of the entire human race" and that it is "united in true faith" (Q & A 54).

Once again, of course, the catechism echoes Scripture. Paul's vision of Christ's future for the church is that "we all attain to the unity of the faith and of the knowledge of the Son of God, to mature manhood, to the measure of the stature of the fulness of Christ" (Eph. 4:13). To the churches addressed in Paul's letter that unity of faith surely stood against the elitist gnostic dogma that threatened them, but it also stood against the enmity that divided Jewish and Gentile Christians. The Jews and the Gentiles were hardly homogeneous. Centuries of racial, political, and religious pride had borne the fruit of enmity. It was not easy for the Jewish

Christian to stop judging and start welcoming Gentiles. It was not easy for the Gentile Christians to stop despising and start accepting Jews. But these former racists, Paul insisted, were and were to be "united in true faith." Christ had made of the two one new humanity in him (Eph. 2:15), and in the grip of the mind of Christ they learned and they cared that the Son of God gathers a community for himself "out of the entire human race." Jew and Gentile, master and slave, rich and poor, male and female—all were and are and are to be one in Christ.

To confess the catechism in a world like this one will make us uneasy about the remnants of social and ethnic homogeneity in our denomination. And it will not permit us to countenance schemes for the "growth" of the church along socially homogeneous lines. The Son of God gathers a community out of the entire human race. It is *his* mission first of all, only graciously entrusted to us. And our participation in his mission must reflect, in both strategies and goals, the victory he has won over the walls of division between races and classes and nations and sexes. Our work must presage the future he has revealed when all will be one in him.

The church's growth into the "measure of the stature of the fulness of Christ" will be measured by its faithfulness to the calling to welcome and serve even those quite unlike us. To say "I am and always will be a living member" of such a community, Christ's community, will affect our social dispositions and intentions toward the black, the poor, the hungry, the women among us. We are one with them, and we are called "readily and cheerfully" to serve and enrich them. The catechism's doctrine of the church, too, is not to be merely memorized but lived.

Since our union with Christ is an active union—since, that is, the acts of God in Jesus Christ and his Spirit form and inform our lives until we conform to his righteousness—to share in Christ who gathers, protects, and preserves a community is to be duty-bound to use our gifts "readily and cheerfully for the service and enrichment of the other members" (Q & A 55). If some are still tempted to read the catechism as an individualistic and introspective confession, this section of the Heidelberg surely should protect and preserve them from that temptation. It is "as members of this community" that we "share in Christ and in all his treasures and gifts" (Q & A 55). And it is as each shares in Christ and in his costly grace that each "should consider it his duty to use his gifts readily and cheerfully for the service and enrichment of the other members" (Q & A 55).

In that memorable line the catechism virtually offers its commentary on 1 Corinthians 12–14. The Corinthian Christian community was a spiritually gifted community. No one—least of all, Paul—denied that. But with subtle pride and selfishness some turned God's gifts into occasions for boasting, envy, and strife. The problem got so bad that the Corinthian church wrote Paul, asking him about the spiritual gifts. Paul's response is found in 1 Corinthians 12–14. To paraphrase, it begins something like this:

> *Now look, friends. You ask about spiritual gifts or about these so-called spiritually gifted people. I don't want you to be stupid about this—or to*

*have the sort of wisdom that can't understand the foolishness of the cross. The
ignorant wisdom of the world might be impressed by the exceptional, the
extraordinary, the ecstatic—but I expected better things from you. You know
that that's what impressed you when you still worshiped in those pagan
temples. Oh, how you oohed and ahed when some ecstatic Sybil murmured
ominous phrases in her mantic trance—even if her gods could not speak a
word. But you must know better now. No one—no matter how ecstatic and
extraordinary and impressive their manner—says 'Jesus be damned!' if he is
gifted by the Spirit of God. And anyone who makes the confession of the church
'Jesus is Lord'—anyone, I say, even the old man you think a clod—is indeed
spiritually gifted.*

*You are not to judge gifts the way the world does. The test is not their
extraordinariness or their ecstacy but their conformity to the pattern of the
cross. The Spirit who comes from God binds us to Jesus, to his cross, and to his
reign. There are many different gifts, many charismata. Note well what I say;
I choose my words carefully. You know that when the emperor celebrates a
birthday or a victory, he gives his troops a charisma, a free gift. It is not a
wage. The troops haven't earned it. They simply receive it from the gratuitous
generosity of the emperor. Your gifts are nothing but charismata. When
Christ ascended on high, he led captivity captive and gave gifts, charismata,
to his troops (Eph. 4:8).*

*How then can you boast about them—as though you had earned
them? And how can you belittle your own gifts, even if unspectacular and
mundane and everyday? How can you envy those with extraordinary gifts as
though any and every gift is not to be received with gratitude?*

*These gifts, then, are not occasions for boasting or for envy. They are
occasions for service, for ministry. According to the pattern laid down by
Christ, the gifts are to be used not for ourselves but for others. As there are
diverse gifts, so there are diverse ministries. You may minister to each other
and to the world in different ways because there are different gifts, but you—
all of you—are ministers because you are all gifted. Let no one boast then
about his knowledge or eloquence or ecstasy. Let every person minister. And
let no one deny the gift and the ministry of simply sharing bread with the
hungry or time with the lonely or a laugh with the disheartened or faith with
the doubting. That, too, is a ministry that the one Spirit gives and demands
and that fits the pattern of our one Lord.*

*Remember, then, that everyday and mundane workings of care and
patience and sharing and hospitality are no less gifts of the Spirit—to be used
readily and cheerfully in the service of others—than the most spectacular
deeds of worship. Indeed the best and the greatest of the gifts is the least
sensational, the most mundane of all—love.*

Then follows, of course, the famous chapter on love, 1 Corinthians
13. This chapter is part of Paul's judgment against the elitist Christians in
Corinth; it points them toward the kind of life where self-glorifying has no
place, where Christians readily and cheerfully serve their neighbors.

Finally, it's worth observing that the catechism presupposes the church as the context for Christian nurture. The whole catechism belongs in the context of the Christian community. It is there that its doctrines are learned—and learned not just by the memory and understanding but as a matter of social life and economic life and political life. It is critically important, then, that the life of the church reflect and image its confession.

The Sacraments and Discipline

The catechism's long section on the sacraments (Qs & As 65–85) may seem remote from this book's interest in the implications of our confession for our life in the world. But if in the catechism the sacraments always point to God's grace, they also always point to our human responsibility. Indeed, precisely because they are signs and seals of the grace by which we participate in Christ, the sacraments remind us of the demanding implications of that participation in Christ.

Baptism initiates us at once into Christ, into the community, and into the Christian life, "so that more and more I become dead to sin and increasingly live a holy and blameless life" (Q & A 70, cf. Qs & As 88–90). We may not cheapen the grace of God signed and sealed in baptism by restricting the meaning of "a holy and blameless life" to certain religious duties. We are to live a holy and blameless commerce, a holy and blameless politics, a holy and blameless consumption. As Donald Bruggink put it, "Baptism, when it is biblically understood as baptism into Christ, also speaks to us about our day-to-day affairs, about the way we treat our wives or husbands, children and/or parents, employers or employees, and all the other people with whom we live in one relation or another."

The Lord's Supper, too, reminds and assures us that we share in Christ and his demanding gifts (Q & A 75). To eat the body and drink the blood means that "we are united more and more to Christ's blessed body" (Q & A 76). It is difficult to express this unity in a figure stronger than the catechism's "flesh of his flesh and bone of his bone" (Q & A 76). This participation is both gift and claim. We are graciously united to "all of his suffering and obedience" (Q & A 79), and we must act in ways that fit that suffering and obedience.

The gift and claim of participation in the Lord's Supper and in the Lord himself are the context for the catechism's discussion of discipline. If we are unwilling to accept the grace and the demands of that union, then we must refrain from the supper. If we are unwilling to accept that participation as grace, if we proudly think we may go on our own, we eat and drink judgment unto ourselves. We must be "displeased" with ourselves because of our sins and "nevertheless trust" that our sins are pardoned by our gracious participation in Christ's suffering and obedience (Q & A 81). And, if we are unwilling to accept that participation as claim, if we slothfully think we need do nothing (or may do anything we like), we eat and drink judgment unto ourselves. Instead we must "desire more and more to strengthen our faith and to lead a better life" (Q & A 81). Those who do not accept this participation as grace and as claim "the Christian church is duty bound to exclude . . . by the official use of the keys of the kingdom, until they reform their lives" (Q & A 82).

The sacrament is God's confirmation of our participation in Christ. And precisely because God confirms that participation to those who receive it as gift and as demand, the church excludes those who refuse to reform their lives. We are accustomed to think introspectively here or in the fairly limited terms of family life, but the catechism gives us no license to restrict the scope of our repentance and reform. The texts used to confirm the catechism's teaching here, in fact, demand that the scope not be restricted. Isaiah 1:16–17 issues these instructions: "Wash yourselves, make yourselves clean; remove the evil of your doings from before my eyes; cease to do evil, learn to do good; seek justice, correct oppression; defend the fatherless, plead for the widow."

Gustavo Gutierrez made the point very forcibly: "There are some Christians among the oppressed and persecuted and others among the oppressors and persecutors. . . . Thus there is occurring a grave and radical confrontation between Christians who suffer injustice and exploitation and those who benefit from the established order. Under these conditions . . . participation in the Eucharist . . . is considered by many to be— for want of the support of an authentic community—an exercise in make-believe."

If that sounds too radical, consult the apostle Paul on the same point. In 1 Corinthians 10 and 11, the chapters repeatedly referred to and echoed by the catechism, Paul rebukes the Corinthians for supposing that the supper is magically effective and not gift and demand at the same time. The point of reference for his rebuke is the Corinthian treatment of the poor (11:17–22 and 33–34); nothing else is mentioned in the context, including any lack of worshipful regard for the sacrament itself. To celebrate the supper without communion, without fellowship, without seeking justice or correcting oppression, without defending the poor or pleading for the powerless is to partake in an "unworthy manner." For each of us to partake introspectively without a sense of being constituted one body in Christ is a misuse of the sacrament. We may not come to the supper without the intentions to share with the poor, to empower the powerless, to end racial injustice and economic exploitation. The scope of church discipline is social and political because our participation in Christ is social and political.

Participation in Christ is produced by the Spirit through the preaching of the gospel and confirmed through our use of the sacraments (Q & A 65). The preaching of the gospel, like the sacraments, is at once gift and demand. It both opens the doors of the kingdom and brings judgment (Q & A 84). Preaching makes explicit the gospel's claims for our social and political life. It announces the gospel as the righteousness of God and, therefore, charges us with the responsibility to seek justice and correct oppression.

In the same way, the mutual admonition of Christian discipline, which first appears as exclusion and judgment, is also grace (Qs & As 84, 85). Discipline, according to the catechism, intends the sinner's repentance. It is, first of all, a mutual responsibility that we accept to and for each other. The church is a community of mutual admonition, a community of sinners who need each other for encouragement and admonition. Moreover, the catechism gives no reason to concentrate admonition exclusively on marital and family problems or to neglect mutual admonition concerning business policies, mortgage policies, political life, and race relations. "The time has come for judgment to begin with the household of God" (1 Peter 4:17).

Is our participation in Christ an active union? Does the action and intention of God in Christ and his Spirit form and inform and reform our life together, our social intentions and dispositions and policies and actions? The time has come to live the catechism.

The Church as a Community of Moral Discourse

There is much here that can strengthen, extend, renew, and reform our vision of the church and for the church. Sharing in Christ makes us a community, a congregation. He gives us our identity and our righteousness, which are his identity and his righteousness. We acknowledge and accept that gift with the sacraments. And with that gift he enables and claims such an identity and such a righteousness. And we acknowledge and accept that demand with the sacraments. That gift and demand enable and require the exercise of discipline and discernment; they enable and require the congregation to be a community of mutual admonition and moral discourse.

That gift and demand enabled the Roman church to be such a community. Paul writes to them, "I myself am satisfied about you, my brethren, that you yourselves are full of goodness, filled with all knowledge, and able to instruct one another" (Rom. 15:14). When Christians met at Rome (or Ephesus or Jerusalem or Corinth or . . .), they talked about and asked their leaders about authority and appropriate dress, about law and the duties of slaves, about love and obedience to Caesar. They were communities of moral discourse. They were, of course, also communities of worship and praise, of therapy and education; when they gathered, they had a number of intentions. But among these was surely their intention to think about, talk about, and pray about their moral responsibilities.

Today the church continues to be a community of moral discourse. Again, it is not only a community of moral discourse. It is also a community of worship, praise, therapy, and education. But surely, when we gather as the people of God, we think about, talk about, and pray about our moral responsibilities, including our social and political responsibilities. We talk about and ask our leaders about authority and women's rights, about law and city government, about love and medical technology.

This is one of the ways in which we stand in the tradition of the earliest Christian communities. There are other ways, of course, other links, but the Christian church is traditionally a community of moral discourse.

The Christian church discourses morally not just out of a sense of tradition, however, but also out of a sense of vocation. We engage in moral discourse today not simply because the Roman Church did many yesterdays ago, but because we continue to be loyal to those convictions and commitments that called forth moral discourse in the past.

The Roman Church was—and was called to be—a community of moral discourse. We are—and are called to be—a community of moral discourse. Why? Because they knew and we know "that our old self was crucified with him so that the sinful body might be destroyed, and we might no longer be enslaved to sin" (Rom. 6:6). We, like the Romans, are called to reflect, pray, and talk about our personal and social responsibilities because of our participation in Christ. "The death he died he died to sin, once for all, but the life he lives he lives to God. So you also must consider yourselves dead to sin and alive to God in Christ Jesus" (Rom. 6:10, 11). The Roman church and our church are called to "be transformed by the renewal of your mind, that you may prove [or discern] what is the will of God, what is good and acceptable and perfect" (Rom. 12:2).

That renewal of our lives and minds takes place in the context of the Christian community, in the context of the church with the Word and sacraments and discipline, in the context of mutual admonition and communal discernment. So Paul tells them (and us) that they (and we) are full of knowledge and goodness and able to instruct one another (Rom. 15:14).

It would be easy to let romantic notions of the glories of the early church exempt us from Paul's description—and so exempt us from the vocation to be a community of moral discourse today. It would be easy—too easy—to say, "Yes, but that was the Roman church. We just are not that gifted with knowledge and goodness." But that line of reasoning is unacceptable.

In the first place, the Roman church was not extraordinarily gifted with knowledge and goodness. They had no extraordinary patience with each other's opinions or even much respect for each other's reasons. Some of the "weak," Paul tells us, judged the "strong." And some of the "strong" despised the "weak." They didn't agree about the place or importance of the law in Christian discernment or about the meaning of Christian freedom. But Paul was satisfied, he says, that they had the resources to be a community of moral discernment.

In the second place, the church's knowledge and goodness are not just the sum of what individual members know or the collection of each individual's good deeds. The church is full of knowledge and goodness because it is the body of Christ. As members of this community, believers one and all share in Christ and in all his knowledge and goodness (cf. Q & A 55). Christ and his Spirit fill the church with all his treasures and gifts, filled even the Roman church with knowledge and goodness, fill even our contemporary church with knowledge and goodness.

The gift of moral discourse demands that we not use what we know that we know or the little good that we do well as reasons to judge or despise our neighbor. Rather, all of our little certainties and virtues are challenged and judged by Christ. All our knowledge is tested by the truth that Christ is and embodies and gives to the church. All our goodness is tested by the perfection that Christ is and embodies and promises to the church. What that means more concretely is that in the church all our political and social and economic and national loyalties are questioned and judged by our loyalty to Christ. For example, in the church our knowledge that "the American way of life" is good is open to question and qualification by the Way, the Truth, and the Life.

We, like the church at Rome, are created as a unique community of moral discourse by our radical loyalty to the God who raised Jesus from the dead. We all live in other communities with values and loyalties: professional societies, labor unions, suburbs, political associations, the country. But all of these values and loyalties must submit, we acknowledge in faith, to the church's confession that Jesus Christ is Lord. All our other loyalties and values must be subjected to his lordship. The vocation to be a community of moral discourse is not earned; it is God's gift and his demand. We may only receive it with gratitude and resolve. The very grace of God that filled the Roman church with knowledge and goodness fills the contemporary church and enables it to be a community of moral discourse and discernment, permits and requires it to bring every political thought and social value and economic loyalty into submission to God.

We have identified certain social intentions as having creedal authorization. But these intentions need to be made more specific. What specifically does the intention to be responsible as an investor to the one God of our comfort (chapter 2) require of a particular congregation? What specific thing may a certain congregation do to live with its intentions to love concretely in a world of selfishness (chapter 3)? What does our responsibility to God the creator, judge, and redeemer in the arena of race relations (chapter 4) require of a particular congregation in a particular place and time? How precisely may our faith's concern for the earth (chapter 5) come to concrete and effective expression? How can our intention of liberation (chapter 6) be given specific force?

The specifics of particular intentions cannot be adequately developed within the pulpit alone. Such a task requires not only theological acumen, moral insight, and imagination but also knowledge of persons, places, opportunities, and obstructions. It is the preacher's role to remind people of God's grace and claims, to call them continually to reestablish themselves on the loyalty that defines the church and on the intentions—including the social intentions—which are implicit in that loyalty (cf. Q & A 84).

Making those intentions specific is not the task of the pastor alone or the ethicist alone. It is the task of the church in discourse. Discourse involves mutual reason-giving and reason-hearing. It involves the diversity of gifts of the congregation—the special skills, the gifts of wisdom, the gifts of creativity, the technical knowledge—all enlightening the way to discern what deeds and words are worthy of the gospel in the place and times we live.

Institutionally, moral discourse can and should take many forms: dialogue after the sermon, study groups, task forces, political workshops and caucuses—all as part of our active union with Christ. The discourse need not result in unanimity, and it probably won't. But mutual admonition and mutual accountability can encourage and help all Christians to bring every political opinion, every social strategy, every economic goal and tactic captive to the Lord Jesus Christ. It is as Richard Mouw said: "If the institutional church can promote an atmosphere in which the tactical diversity of Christians in politics can be undergirded by a common concern for Christian obedience and a commitment to sharing together the ways different persons seek to be faithful disciples, we can have a legitimate hope that those efforts will be more effectively coordinated into a harmonious showing forth of the glory of God."

If we can see this vision of the church, if we can receive with gratitude both the gift and the demand of God, then perhaps the church will look less like an archaic museum piece to some of our contemporaries and more like a confident community that knows why it exists and why it acts, more like the very image of its Lord, actively participating in his suffering and in his reign.

Acknowledgments and Suggestions for Further Reading

The quotation from Lewis Smedes at the head of the chapter comes from his *Union with Christ* (revised edition of *All Things Made New*; Grand Rapids: Wm. B. Eerdmans, 1970, 1983), p. 92. The book is a very valuable resource for further study of membership in Christ.

The Sandberg poem is "Prayers of Steel." It can be found in *Harvest Poems*, 1910–1960 (New York: Harcourt, Brace & World, 1960), p. 50. On the place of the church in the catechism and the place of the catechism in the church, see Howard Hageman, "The Catechism in Christian Nurture," Bard Thomson, et al., *Essays on the Heidelberg Catechism* (Philadelphia: United Church Press, 1963), especially pp. 164–166, 176–177.

On the sacraments see Donald Bruggink, "The Holy Sacraments" in *Guilt, Grace and Gratitude* (New York: The Half Moon Press, 1963). The quotation is from page 146.

The quotation of Gustavo Gutierrez is from his *A Theology of Liberation* (London: SCM Press, 1974), p. 8.

On the church as a community of moral discourse, see further James M. Gustafson, *The Church as Moral Decision-Maker* (Philadelphia: Pilgrim Press, 1970), and Richard Mouw, *Political Evangelism* (Grand Rapids: Wm. B. Eerdmans, 1973), pp. 83–85. The quote of Mouw is from page 85.

Discussion Questions for Chapter 7

1. Do you agree that our union with Christ is better described as an active union than a mystical union? What's the difference? How does the catechism treat union with Christ?

2. Read Revelation 21:1–8. Is Christ's promise—"Behold, I make all things new"—in the future or in the present or both? See also 2 Corinthians 5:17 and Galatians 6:15.

   Discuss what this promise means. What, for example, is renewed? Nature? Technology? The relationship between people and nature? The relationship between persons of differing cultures, classes, races, sexes? And who is the agent of renewal? Christ? The Holy Spirit? The church? You?

   How can we believe in this renewal when so much is broken and spoiled by sin in our world? How can we expect the world to believe it? Is the promise a comfort or a burden or both?

3. Paul's treatment of gifts in the community in 1 Corinthians 12–14 can be summarized in three rules:
   a) To each their own
   b) for the common good
   c) according to the pattern of Christ
   Show how the use of a specific spiritual gift could illustrate the three criteria above.

   What gifts are evident in your group and how are they being used for the common good? Perhaps each group member could identify one gift of another member and tell how it promotes the common good of the congregation.

   Also, or instead of the above, take some time to privately identifv your own gifts and think about how they could be used for the common good. Do not neglect gifts which are unspectacular and mundane, or gifts which are relevant to the social and political and economic ministry of the church.

4. Paul tells certain women in Corinth not to discard the veil when they pray and prophesy in church (1 Cor. 11:2–16). Do you agree that Paul is suggesting that these women be allowed to use their gifts in the church's worship, but that they must use them according to the pattern of Christ—that is, in ways that serve the common good rather than exalt themselves? What bearing, if any, does this interpretation have on the way we use this passage in the church today? What should we say to the gifted women among us? Should what we say to gifted women be any different than what we say to gifted men?

5. Choose from among the following questions on the Lord's Supper:

In what ways, if any, is the Lord's Supper a political statement? If we are not sharing food and drink with the hungry, if we are not doing what must and can be done to secure for others these elementary supplies, may we come to the Lord's table with a good conscience? In your discussion refer to Gustavo Gutierrez's remark quoted above.

Discuss this statement by John Calvin: "We shall benefit very much from the Sacrament if this thought is impressed and engraved upon our minds: . . . that, as no part of our body is touched by any feeling of pain which is not spread among all the rest, so we ought not to allow a brother to be affected by any evil, without being touched with compassion for him" (4, xvii, 38). How would such a thought help us "benefit from the sacrament?"

Read 1 Corinthians 11:17–34. What seems to have been the problem with the celebration of the communal meal in Corinth? Are there any similar problems in the celebration of the Lord's Supper in our world?

6. Would you call your church "a community of moral discourse"? Why or why not? In discussing this basic question, think about the ways your church nurtures and sponsors mutual admonition. Perhaps you have suggestions for new ways in which your church could institutionalize communal discourse and discernment. In such discourse it is not important to agree about *everything*, but what things *are* important to agree about?

Paul's little letter to Philemon was also addressed to "the church in your house" (v. 2), a church that surely included slaves and to which Philemon, the slave-owner, also had to give an account. Does your congregation include the hungry, the oppressed, the poor? Does it have contact with them? How is this important to the quality of the moral discourse that occurs among us?

98

8

GRATITUDE AND GOD'S PERMISSIONS

Q. We have been delivered
 from our misery
 by God's grace alone through Christ
 and not because we have earned it:
 Why then must we still do good?

A. To be sure, Christ has redeemed us by his blood.
 But we do good because
   Christ by his Spirit is also renewing us to be like himself,
   so that in all our living
   we may show that we are thankful to God
     for all he has done for us,
   and so that he may be praised through us.

 And we do good
   so that we may be assured of our faith by its fruits,
   and so that by our godly living
     our neighbors may be won over to Christ.
                    —Heidelberg Catechism Q & A 86

Q. But can those converted to God
 obey these commandments perfectly?

A. No.
 In this life even the holiest
 have only a small beginning of this obedience.

Nevertheless, with all seriousness of purpose,
they do begin to live
according to all, not only some,
of God's commandments.

—Heidelberg Catechism Q & A 114

I will put my law within them, and I will write it upon their hearts; and I will
be their God, and they shall be my people.

—Jeremiah 31:33

The third and principal use, which pertains more closely to the proper purpose
of the law, finds its place among believers in whose hearts the Spirit of God
already lives and reigns.

—John Calvin, Institutes, *2, vii, 12*

What drives the Christian to love and obedience is thankfulness. This gives to
the moral life a characteristic note of joy. Appreciative of God's mercy,
thankful for his unspeakable gift, happy in his gracious conferments, the
Christian seeks with might and main to show forth his praises and to do his
will. Living in the context of grace, he no longer strives to reach a heaven that
is in any case beyond his reach; resting from his labors in Christ's embrace, he
seeks in all things to please him. . . .
In this frame of reference morality loses all its hardness and harshness. Duties
are no longer onerous. The law is certainly still there, but it is no longer con-
templated as a code of perfection that no mortal can ever satisfy; it is
contemplated as a gracious prescription, supplying a happy and thankful
man with helpful directives concerning how to satisfy someone whom it is his
deepest desire to please.

—Henry Stob, Ethical Reflections

THE CATECHISM KNOWS that the context of the law is grace. God does not give the law as a tyrant who would extort obedience, cracking his whip to get an unruly humanity to behave. He gives the law as the deliverer, as the one who brought us out of the house of bondage, as the one who acts to save his world. He wills the law because he wills our participation in his righteousness, because he wills our flourishing. We misinterpret and misuse the law at this point if we use it simply to judge and condemn.

Of course, the same law previously disclosed our misery (Q & A 3), but we are no longer the same people. We live in a new situation—namely, in Christ. We have been brought from misery into deliverance. So "why then must we still do good?" (Q & A 86). The catechism allows this question without sympathizing with it. And, in answering, it insists that our deliverance, our participation in Christ's righteousness, is our renewal as well as our redemption. "Christ by his Spirit is also renewing us to be like himself, so that in all our living we may show that we are thankful to God for all he has done for us, and so that he may be praised through us" (Q & A 86).

The catechism's point is that we do good not because we *must*, but because we *may*. Our participation in Christ is our permission in "all our living" (Q & A 86)—in our marrying, working, saving, spending, managing, consuming, playing, politicking—to show that we are thankful and to praise God. The law is the shape of God's permission to live a new life. To receive God's grace is to receive this permission—and to refuse this permission is to refuse participation in Christ. "It is impossible for those grafted into Christ by true faith not to produce fruits of gratitude" (Q & A 64, cf. Q & A 87).

It is true that "even the very best we do in this life is imperfect and stained with sin" (Q & A 62). And it is true that "in this life even the holiest have only a small beginning of this obedience" (Q & A 114). Nevertheless, God does grant his permission. Our participation in Christ is our renewal to be like him (Q & A 86). In Christ the old self dies and the new comes to life (Q & A 88), so that we hate sin (Q & A 89) and "delight to do every kind of good" (Q & A 90). God gives permission, and his people "do begin to live according to all, not only some, of God's commandments" (Q & A 114).

The commandments (or permissions) of the Decalogue can only be treated in an introductory and summary fashion in the next two chapters. The whole book might have examined the catechism's treatment of the Law and the ways in which the catechism received God's permission to live a new life in the real life of the sixteenth century. The catechism applies the Law to its own time, after all, to its own social and political and religious situation. The first commandment is taken to forbid prayers to saints (Q & A 94); the second, pictures in church (Q & A 98). In the third commandment the catechism distinguishes itself from the Anabaptists by allowing certain oaths (Q & A 101) for the sake of justice. The fourth commandment is taken to require the maintenance of education for the gospel ministry (Q & A 103). Police power is justified in the exposition of the sixth (Q & A 105). The eighth commandment is applied to counterfeit money and excessive interest (Q & A 110); the ninth, to slander and condemnation without due process and just cause (Q & A 112).

Sometimes the catechism's application to the sixteenth century seems archaic and strained today; more often, profound and provocative. But we need not—and may not—simply repeat the catechism's applications. We must do for our own time and place what the catechism did for its. We must receive and announce God's permissions to live a new life in the twentieth century. For that task the catechism remains a standard, and to that task the next two chapters will be given.

The first four commandments have to do with "what our relation to God should be" (Q & A 93). But that doesn't mean the catechism treats them as socially irrelevant. Quite the contrary, the Heidelberg sets our relation with God in the context of this world and this history.

The First Permission

Q. *What does the Lord require*
   in the first commandment?

A. *That I, not wanting to endanger my very salvation,*
   avoid and shun
      all idolatry, magic, superstitious rites,
      and prayer to saints or to other creatures.

  That I sincerely acknowledge the only true God,
     trust him alone,
     look to him for every good thing
      humbly and patiently,
     love him, fear him, and honor him
      with all my heart.

  In short,
     that I give up anything
     rather than go against his will in any way.
             —*Heidelberg Catechism Q & A 94*

"Hear, O Israel: the Lord our God is one Lord" (Deut. 6:4). That ancient Jewish confession of faith, called the Shema, was an incredible thing to say. All Israel's neighbors knew, or thought they knew, that the universe was a jungle of warring powers—some good, some evil, but all demanding to be pleased and placated. But Israel said, "The Lord our God is one Lord." It is important to observe, I think, that the confession was practical rather than speculative; that is, before the Israelites denied the real existence of other gods, they acknowledged that only one deserved to be worshiped. Other gods might exist, but only one is Lord, only one deserves our ultimate loyalty. The commandment says, after all, "Have no other gods before me."

The Scriptures reveal a lively struggle between God and the gods, between God on the one side and Baal and Marduk and Bel and Zeus and all the principalities and powers on the other. The struggle continues and the first commandment permits us to enlist on the Lord's side.

When God called Abraham out of Ur, he called him to turn from idols and to serve a living God. When God rescued his people from Egypt, he humiliated the Egyptian gods and their priests with the plagues. When the people entered Canaan, they learned the arts of agriculture from the natives. And since in Canaan the art of agriculture involved homage to Baal, for a time God's people were confused. But at Mt. Carmel God won a great victory, and all the people shouted "The Lord, he is God" (1 Kings 18:40) and went home free to farm without worrying about placating or pleasing Baal, free to farm before the face of God alone. So the Israelite farmers left a strip unharvested at the edge of their fields for the gleaners, for the poor, but no longer strived to insure fertility by placating Baal.

Three hundred years later, far from the land of Canaan, in exile in Babylon, the antagonist looked far more powerful. Baal had claimed power over fertile fields and fertile wombs, but the gods of the Babylonians claimed power over life and death, over victory and defeat. There by the waters of Babylon the Israelites "sat down and wept" (Ps. 137:1), for it looked as though Marduk, the god of light, the chief of the Babylonian gods, had won. The Babylonians, of course, were soon defeated by the Medes and Persians, and a certain King Cyrus quietly wrote an edict permitting the Jews to go home to Jerusalem. It might escape our notice as God's victory save for the prophet who called Cyrus "God's anointed" and by whom God announced again, "I am the Lord, and there is no other. . . . I form light and create darkness" (Isa. 45:1–7). Marduk, the god of light, was shown up by the one who has power over light and darkness.

Back in Jerusalem, the Jews sang the Lord's song with joy. Did Baal still claim power over fertile fields and fertile wombs? Psalm 95:3 praises God as "a great King above all gods." Did the gods of the nations still claim power over freedom and slavery, victory and defeat? The psalms contemptuously refer to them as "nothings." Did the gods still license oppression? Psalm 82 has God assemble them, judge them for their injustice, and sentence them: "You shall die like men." So God rescued the weak and needy.

Then climactically and decisively the struggle shifted to Calvary, to a miserable hill outside Jerusalem. A certain Jesus hung there and died like any man. People mocked and taunted: "He trusted in God, let God deliver him now." And the powers thought they had bested him. But this is the good news: God delivered him. God raised him from the dead and showed himself to be powerful over sin and death, over the principalities and powers and dominions. When God raised Jesus from the dead, he set him "at his right hand in the heavenly places, far above all rule and authority and power and dominion" (Eph. 1:20–21). So Paul proclaimed to Gentile as well as Jew, "Hear, O Gentiles! The Lord our God is one Lord," and demanded on the strength of that confession one community of Jew and Gentile (Rom. 3:29–30, Eph. 2:13–22).

The conflict between God and the gods had to do—and still has to do—with such mundane and "secular" things as farming and fertility, international politics and defense, justice for the poor and powerless, and community for different races. The confession that there is one God and the commandment to have no other gods before him permit us to live our lives—all of them—in his grace and for his glory. The first commandment permits us to live all of life without the distortion of divinized phenomena or causes or powers or nations. As the catechism says, it requires—or permits—us to "acknowledge the only true God, trust him alone, look to him for every good thing humbly and patiently, love him, fear him, and honor him with all my heart" and with all my life and all our common life. The powers may no longer claim our ultimate loyalty. None of the things which we have or invent and in which we put our trust may lay claim to our ultimate loyalty—not our nation, not our racial heritage, not our economic status, not sex, not technology, not public opinion, not any of the things that influence and sometimes dominate our lives without ever being fully visible.

The struggle continues, of course. But the victory has been won. All the old and new deifications of nature or sex or military power or national interest or wealth or technology or a race or a class hopelessly continue the struggle against God. We are permitted to live quite secular lives to the glory of God and the benefit of our neighbors. That's the permission of the first commandment. To disobey, to suppose anything else is permitted us, is to submit again to a yoke of bondage, to idolatry.

The Second Permission

Q. What is God's will for us
in the second commandment?

A. That we in no way make any image of God
nor worship him in any other way
than he has commanded in his Word.
—*Heidelberg Catechism Q & A 96*

The second commandment, the prohibition of images, permits us to depend on God and his Word. The neighbors of Israel focused on cultic images at worship, but Israel was directed to God's Word. Moses reminded the Israelites that at Horeb (or Sinai) they had seen no form; they had only heard a voice. That's the way it is to be, Moses said: no images, only attentive listening to his Word—the Word of covenant and its law (Deut. 4:15–19, referred to by Q & A 96).

It's a hard lesson. Again and again the people needed to be reminded of it. Samuel reminded Saul of it in 1 Samuel 15:22–23, (another of the references of Q & A , 96): sacrifices can be mere images, God delights in obedience. The prophets also were prepared to reject the worship of the people when it did not lead to justice (e.g., Isa. 1:12–17, Micah 6:6–8, Amos 5:21–24).

The catechism reminds us of the same lesson, permitting us to depend on God and his Word, and so to live. We sometimes refuse this permission, too, paying homage to some cultic image, the Bible, the sacrament, the institutional church, even success and prosperity as proof of our virtue, while we neglect obedience to his Word. "And what does the Lord require of you but to do justice, and to love kindness, and to walk humbly with your God?" (Mic. 6:8).

The prohibition of images is the flip side of God's prohibition of idols. God is the only Lord of this world, and he can be met only where he chooses to reveal himself. God cannot be captured by an image or a concept, but he freely came to Israel in her history and in his messengers. They could never define him; they could only report his works and his words. The prohibition of images set Israelite life and worship in quite a different context from that of her neighbors. Israel had to depend—and was permitted to depend—on God and his Word.

With many wonderful stories the Israelites reminded themselves how difficult and delightful it is to depend on God, what costly comfort it is to depend on God. One such story is the story of the ark in battle (1 Sam. 4:1–7:4). Imagine an old man telling his grandson the story:

> I remember it like it was yesterday. Things were quite different then. Why, you don't even think of the Philistines as a threat. But they were. We had just lost a battle, and it looked bad. What could we do? Someone came up with the bright idea of bringing the ark of the Lord into the second battle. Surely the presence of the Lord would reverse our fortunes and insure our victory in the second battle. So we went and got the ark and brought it into the camp, noisily congratulating ourselves on this stroke of genius. Rumors of our new strategy reached the Philistines, and rumors of Philistine fear reached back to us. We began the battle confidently, but it became a disaster. We lost worse than before. And the Philistines captured the ark of the Lord.
>
> I'm ashamed to tell you this—not because I fled that day, but because of what we tried to do. We made the ark into an image. It was a symbol of God's presence, but we tried to confine him there and to manipulate him to serve our ends. We wanted to be God's lord instead of allowing him to be our Lord. But God would not oblige. He would not be domesticated by us or used for our success.
>
> The Philistines didn't understand, of course. They thought they had won a victory over God. They took the ark back to Ashdod and put it in the temple of their god Dagon, boasting all the while. The next day Dagon laid in pieces. The Lord our God won a great victory over Dagon and over the Philistines. And they are no longer a threat.
>
> But, listen to me now, my boy. The reason I tell you this story is that you may know that you must serve God, not seek by images to manipulate him into serving you. This monarchy thing may work, but not if we try to use God for the success of our little political causes. It will work only if we and our little causes serve God.

The old man and the catechism remind us of the contrast between cultic images and the Word, between the attempt to control God, to achieve some mastery over him, and the willingness to be controlled and mastered by God. Calvin, too, contended that image-making was the human effort to domesticate God and that such an effort contradicted the fundamental principle that "God himself is the sole and proper witness of himself" (1, xi, 1). But God will not be domesticated. He will not be controlled. He will not be used for our success in battle or in business, in politics or in sex. He is the Lord, and his lordship includes our battles and our business, our politics and our sex.

The second commandment is the announcement that God will not permit us to be his lords, but he will permit us to have him as our Lord. He permits us not to be served but to serve him and therefore our neighbor. He gives us the liberating permission to recognize and celebrate his authority—not to trust our graven images, but to trust him and his Word. He gives us the freedom not to "try to be wiser than God" (Q & A 98), but to worship him as he has commanded in his Word:

> *Is not this the fast that I choose: to loose the bonds of wickedness, to undo the thongs of the yoke, to let the oppressed go free, and to break every yoke? Is it not to share your bread with the hungry, and bring the homeless poor unto your house? (Isa. 58: 6–7)*

The Third Permission

Q. What is God's will for us
*   in the third commandment?*

A. That we neither blaspheme nor misuse the name of God
*   by cursing, perjury, or unnecessary oaths,*
*   nor share in such horrible sins*
*   by being silent bystanders.*

* In a word, it requires*
*   that we use the holy name of God*
*   only with reverence and awe,*
*   so that we may properly*
*   confess him,*
*   pray to him,*
*   and praise him in everything we do and say.*
*   —Heidelberg Catechism Q & A 99*

In its exposition of the third commandment the catechism announces God's sovereignty. We have sometimes trivialized the commandment by restricting its application to profanity—"the effort of a feeble mind to express itself forcefully," said the sign in the barber shop I visited as a child. I do not intend to make such profanity appear trivial, but too often my reaction to it as a child was: "Oh, that's the sin drill sergeants commit. I thank you, God, that I and my parents and my barber are not like others." We ought not read the catechism in such a way. It intends to guide our gratitude, not license our pride.

Today names are basically an aesthetic matter. Parents choose names that sound nice. But in the biblical world things were different. The name of something signified its very essence—and to know the name was to have power over the person or thing. When Adam and Eve named the animals, it signified that men and women had power over the animals. The implication of names in the Bible is not unimportant to the significance of the third commandment.

At the burning bush, when Moses was charged to go down to Egypt, he wanted to know the name of the one who sent him. The one who called him answered, "I AM WHO I AM. . . . Say this to the people of Israel, 'I AM has sent me to you' " (Ex. 3:14). Why did God refuse to answer more explicitly? The God who had forbidden images would not give humans power over himself. He would not be captured and confined and made subject to a man or a nation by a name. Instead the people were to subject themselves to him. They were to depend on God, his work, and his Word. And yet there is a name: "I AM WHO I AM."

The God who called Moses was—and is—at work in history, and he called Moses to that work. The revelation of his name did not give Moses power over him. Rather it enlisted Moses—as it enlists us—in his work. The prohibition against blasphemy and the misuse of his name is our permission to make his work our work, his mission our mission, his passion our passion. So he is blasphemed not merely in speech but in history, not merely in what we "say" but in what we "do" in this profane world where he is at work (cf. Q & A 99).

We misuse his name when we worship on Sunday and seek only our own prosperity and power on Monday. We take his name in vain when we piously pray for racial justice without being willing to help change hiring and firing practices where we work. We blaspheme by acknowledging "God intends to feed the hungry" without supporting ecclesiastical and political action for the relief of hunger. The commandment frees us from such duplicity and permits us to "confess him, pray to him, and praise him in everything we do and say" (Q & A 99). The commandment frees us to hallow God's name, to "direct all our living" by all that "shines forth" from God's works, his "power, wisdom, kindness, justice, mercy, and truth" (Q & A 122).

Confession of faith and prayer and praise and worship are not ways to get things out of God. If we use them in that way, they become graven images. They are rather ways of participating in the work and passion of God; therefore, to "properly confess him, pray to him, and praise him" spills over into our whole life, into "everything we do and say" (Q & A 99). To name his name "with reverence and awe" enlists us in his service and the service of our neighbors. The third commandment permits us to live, like Moses, as servants of God's intentions of liberation. It frees us to "do everything in the name of the Lord Jesus, giving thanks to God the Father through him" (Col. 3:17).

The catechism's curious treatment of the command in Q & A 101 begins to make some sense in this light. The question is "But may we swear an oath in God's name if we do it reverently?", and the answer understands

107

the commandment against swearing to permit us to swear, to take an oath, where truth and the neighbor's good require it. We may swear, the catechism says "when the government demands it, or when necessity requires it, in order to maintain and promote truth and trustworthiness for God's glory and our neighbor's good" (Q & A 101).

The catechism does not treat the commandment itself as a graven image, as a rule to gain a calculable righteousness for ourselves. It treats the commandment as our permission to hallow his name, to "direct all our living" by God's intentions. God intends truth and trustworthiness and the neighbor's good. So we may—and only may—name his name in promoting truth and trustworthiness and helping our neighbor. To name his name permits us to serve God and our neighbor. And to name his name permits nothing else. Only so do we use his holy name "with reverence and awe" (Q & A 99).

Finally, we should note the catechism's appreciation for government (Q & A 101). Unlike the Anabaptist confessions of the sixteenth century, the catechism does not prohibit oaths in court; it has a positive regard for them. But if oaths *are* permitted in government and in courts, the catechism implies, then these institutions, too, are enlisted in the service of God's intentions of truth, trustworthiness, and our neighbor's good. A government without a modicum of integrity or a court system with different process and punishment for rich and poor or for black and white itself stands under the judgment of blasphemy. And we may not be "silent bystanders" (Q & A 99) to that blasphemy. We are permitted and enlisted by the third commandment to seek integrity and justice. To refuse that permission also in our political responsibilities is to name God's holy name without reverence and awe.

The Fourth Permission

Q. What is God's will for us
   in the fourth commandment?

A. First,
      that the gospel ministry and education for it be maintained,
      and that, especially on the festive day of rest,
      I regularly attend the assembly of God's people
      to learn what God's Word teaches,
      to participate in the sacraments,
      to pray to God publicly,
      and to bring Christian offerings for the poor.

   Second,
      that every day of my life
         I rest from my evil ways,

let the Lord work in me through his Spirit,
  and so begin already in this life
the eternal Sabbath.

—Heidelberg Catechism Q & A 103

In the fourth commandment God does not exact legalistic observance; he rather permits us to be a community celebrating and responding to his grace. Such a community is led into education and relief as well as into worship.

It is always a little startling to find the catechism say that by the fourth commandment God wills "that the gospel ministry and education for it be maintained" (Q & A 103). The commandment is addressing matters as everyday as providing an equitable wage for the minister, as socially significant as the establishment and support of colleges and seminaries. The catechism is interested not in giving us cause to judge our neighbors but in helping us respond gratefully to God's deliverance. It is guidance for a life of praise—and part of that praise is maintaining places like Calvin College and Seminary, Hope College and Western Seminary, Princeton University and Seminary, Westminster Seminary, and the like.

The command—or permission—to "regularly attend the assembly of God's people" (Q & A 103) is less surprising. But it is no less socially significant. The sabbath commandment permits us to be part of a fellowship, part of God's family, which assembles periodically "to learn what God's Word teaches, to participate in the sacraments, to pray to God publicly, and to bring Christian offerings for the poor" (Q & A 103). The catechism echoes Acts 2:42: "They devoted themselves to the apostles' teaching and fellowship, to the breaking of bread and the prayers."

The sabbath commandment gives us the vocation to stand in this tradition of that earliest church. There, with men and women gathered in their working clothes, Peter or John or Andrew would remember words that Jesus had spoken or things Jesus had done. Once, I imagine, when some of the community were grumbling about the new woman of unpleasant reputation who was coming to their gathering, John told the group about a long, hot, wearying walk the disciples took one day just so Jesus could talk with just such a woman. Jesus told her, John recalled, about living water. After that these early Christians were probably a little ashamed and, instead of grumbling, welcomed the woman into their common life.

And what a common life it was! They cared for each other. They prayed for each other. They served each other. They even pooled their pitiful little wages. The woman they had formerly despised became the recipient of their gifts—and not just this woman, but all the poor. The Christian church soon put the empire to shame by providing food and shelter for the poor.

And they broke bread together. Peter would take a loaf of bread and break it—and it would seem his heart would break with it. Whether it broke with joy or with pain, one was never quite certain. But he would pass the loaf along, and all were quite certain that something more than bread was being shared. For here wounds were healed, here rudeness and self-ishness were forgiven, here a community was restored. It was as though Christ himself had walked into the room.

And they prayed together. One time someone broke into the room and announced that James was dead and Simon Peter was now in Herod's prison. That day there must have been an anxious feeling in the con-gregation, a silence not of praise but of doubt. God's cause seemed to have lost ground. And who would be next? Then an old man began to pray. He recited the words he had learned long ago in the synagogue, "Lord thou hast been our dwelling place in all generations . . . ," and as he prayed his voice gained strength and the congregation gained courage. For these people up against the pressures and obligations of the Christian life, prayer was no pious duty; it was an utter necessity. Prayer apart from involvement in life and its obligations quickly can degenerate into a graven image. But these people were not trying to get things out of God. They were not trying to control God. They were getting themselves aligned with the cause of God; they were allowing God to control them.

The catechism says that the fourth command calls and enables us to be just such a community. God frees us from our individualism and makes us members of a people, permitting us to share a common life.

According to the catechism, the fourth command permits us "to bring Christian offerings for the poor." The catechism evidently sees that the sabbath legislation of the Old Testament—including sabbatical years and years of Jubilee (cf. Lev. 25)—had very explicit social implications. (The social implications of the fourth commandment itself are clearer in Deuteronomy than in Exodus.) Calvin, too, had recognized them in his ex-position of the fourth commandment. Part of God's intention with the fourth command, Calvin said, was "to give a day of rest to servants and those who are under the authority of others, in order that they should have some respite from toil" (2, viii, 28). The catechism recognizes, along with the Old Testament and John Calvin, that our permission to celebrate the Lord's Day is at the same time our permission to side with the poor, to seek their rest and well-being, to prevent them from being exploited and used.

The catechism, finally, takes the fourth commandment to permit us to begin already in this life the eternal Sabbath of God's reign. It finds in the fourth commandment all the grace and duty of gospel and takes it to announce costly comfort, the catechism's theme. So, even while it permits us a "festive day of rest," it is not content with any compartmentalization of life into Sunday and the rest of the week. "Every day of my life" (Q & A 103) belongs totally to God. Sunday is a foretaste of God's reign, but all our life, including our social and political life, belongs under his reign.

In All Our Living

The catechism treats the law in the context of God's grace. The law is God's announcement that he has given us permission to live genuinely human lives, thankful lives, lives that praise God in "all our living" (Q & A 86). The first four commandments have to do with "what our relation to God should be" (Q & A 93), but they are not therefore socially irrelevant. Quite the contrary, our relation to God is set in the context of this world and this history. Our duties toward God ever call our attention to our social responsibilities.

The first commandment liberated us from the distortion of divinized phenomena or causes or powers or nations and permitted us to live quite secular lives to the glory of God and the benefit of our neighbors.

The second commandment liberated us from graven images, from trying to use God for our ends, from trying to make God serve us, and permitted us to serve him and to depend on him and his Word.

The third commandment liberated us from trivial religion and permitted us to praise God's name in everything we do and say—indeed, to seek integrity, justice, and our neighbor's good.

The fourth commandment made us a community celebrating and responding to God, and it permitted us to rest in the costly comfort of his lordship, attending to such social responsibilities as education and relief.

So our relation to God, established by God, permits us to be engaged in his struggle against the powers and graven images and blasphemy. That struggle occurs on many different fronts: religious, political, cultural. Our struggle with these temptations is part of God's struggle with and for the world. He has already won the decisive battle in Jesus Christ. And our obedience is set, on the one hand, in the context of our participation in him and, on the other hand, in the context of our own social setting.

A story is told of a rather "comfortable" church, a beautiful church on High St. One of the church's most prized possessions was a stained glass window that read "Glory to God in the Highest." Most of the church's resources went into keeping the building splendid and the rabble, who lived around it, outside.

One day a young boy threw a rock, and—whether by chance or by providence, you may judge—it shattered the little window containing the "e." Suddenly the stained glass window announced what that congregation's task really was: "Glory to God in the High st."

The window, sadly, was fixed. But it's the kind of reminder the church always needs. There is no glorifying God in the highest without glorifying him on High Street. God has freed us to live our secular social lives to his honor, for his glory, and for our neighbor's good.

Appendix on the "Practical Syllogism"

Question 86 has been the subject of a good deal of controversy, as much in sociology as in theology. The claim that "we do good so that we may be assured of our faith by its fruits" (Q & A 86) has been accused of providing a so-called "practical syllogism," by which we gain certainty of our election on the basis of our good works.

It was the thesis of sociologist Max Weber's *The Protestant Ethic and the Spirit of Capitalism* that in the Reformed movement this "practical syllogism" worked to make financial "success" the proof of election. As a result, the movement provided a religious incentive to the growth of capitalism and to the unrestricted, voluntary, self-initiated economic behavior on which its growth depended.

Permit me two modest observations about the thesis of Weber. First, it is historically overdrawn. There were other causes of the modern capitalistic spirit, not least of which was the industrialization wrought by the invention of the steam engine. Second, there were countervailing tendencies within Calvinism itself. Economics may be "freed" from traditional authorities by Calvinism, but it is not freed from the order God gives and demands. The new order in Calvinism includes concerns for equity and justice and community in the economic order, concerns that always tend to be uneasy with with the inequities, injustices, and individualism of free-market capitalism.

Of this second point, Calvin's letter on usury is an interesting example. Calvin was among the first great leaders of public opinion to reject the traditional opinion that the Bible forbids the loaning of money with interest. His opinion surely worked to "free" economics from traditional authorities. But he restricted interest-taking at a number of points. His general principle was "that usury must be judged not by a particular passage of Scripture but simply by the rules of equity" and that "usury is not wholly forbidden among us, except it be repugnant both to justice and to charity." On the basis of those principles Calvin restricted the practice of lending: loans to the poor, for example, were to be made without expectation of interest. So the capitalist tendency in Calvinism, a tendency Weber called attention to, sometimes is and always should be limited and restricted by Calvinism's concern for conformity to a new order of equity and justice and community.

Theologically, some have argued that the practical syllogism and Q & A 86 direct our attention away from Christ and to ourselves and that this stands in contradiction to the catechism's reliance upon the grace of God alone. But the catechism does not make the believer's life the foundation for certainty. How could it when "even the very best we do in this life is imperfect and stained with sin" (Q & A 62, cf. Q & A 114)? This recognition of our imperfection cautions us not only against all self-righteousness but also against weighing and calculating our righteousness as proof of our faith.

Christ and his righteousness remain the foundation. The believer and the believer's life, however, have real participation in that foundation. The point of Q & A 86 is not to direct our attention away from Christ to ourselves and our calculable righteousness; there is no comfort in that. The point is rather to call our attention to the intimate connection, the active union, between the believer and Christ's righteousness. The seriousness of sanctification is understood not apart from Christ but as a participation in Christ, the foundation and reality of the new life.

Acknowledgments and Suggestions for Further Reading

It is worth observing that in Calvin's Strassburg liturgy, the law was sung following the words of pardon. The context of the law in grace and praise was neatly captured by such liturgical practice. See Howard Hageman's "The Law in the Liturgy" in *God and the Good*, edited by C. Orlebeke and L. Smedes (Grand Rapids: Wm. B. Eerdmans, 1975), pp. 25–35. The quotation of Henry Stob at the beginning of the chapter is from his *Ethical Reflections*, p. 78.

On the Decalogue itself the scholarly study of J. J. Stamm and M. D. Andrews, *The Ten Commandments in Recent Research* (London: SCM Press, 1967), may be of interest to readers with some training in biblical studies. Calvin's treatment of the Decalogue (2, vii and viii) is still among the very best resources. The collection of sermons edited by Michael De Vries, *Thy Way is My Way* (Toronto: Credo Publishing Co., 1967) provides some very thoughtful treatments of several of the commandments.

On the theme of "the principalities and powers" a good deal has been written. A good place to begin is Hendrikus Berkhof's *Christ and the Powers* (Scottsdale: Herald Press, 1962). One may also wish to consult Albert van den Heuvel's *These Rebellious Powers* (Naperville, Ill.: SCM, 1965) and Richard Mouw's *Politics and the Biblical Drama* (Grand Rapids: Wm. B. Eerdmans, 1976), pp. 85–116.

John H. Leith has written an interesting piece entitled "Calvin's Polemic Against Idolatry" in *Soli Deo Gloria: New Testament Studies in Honor of William Childs Robinson*, edited by J. McDowell Richards (Richmond: John Knox Press, 1968), pp. 111–124.

In question 2 below, the quotation of W. Harry Jellema is from "On Idolatry," *Christianity Today*, Oct. 13, 1961, p. 38.

The extended note on the "practical syllogism" referred to Max Weber's *The Protestant Ethic and the Spirit of Capitalism* (New York: Charles Scribner's Sons, 1958). Fine discussion of the Weber thesis may be found in *Protestantism, Capitalism and Social Science: The Weber Thesis Controversy*, edited by Robert W. Green (2nd edition; Lexington, Mass.: D.C. Heath and Company, 1973). The outstanding study by David Little, *Religion, Order, and Law* (New York: Harper & Row, 1969), provides a measured defense of Weber's thesis. Calvin's letter on usury is entitled "De Usuris Responsum" and can be found in *Usury Laws* (*Economic tracts;* New York: Society for Political Education, 1880–1881), pp. 32–36. The theological discussion of the practical syllogism is surveyed by G. C. Berkouwer in his *Divine Election* (Grand Rapids: Wm. B. Eerdmans, 1960), pp. 278–306.

Discussion Questions for Chapter 8

1. Do you think it's a good idea to talk about the commandments as "permissions"? Why or why not? Consider whether permissions are as serious a matter as commandments and whether the catechism itself allows us to talk about the commandments as permissions. Why do you think the author uses the language of "permission" rather than the language of "commandment"? Does it make any difference?

2. The catechism defines *idolatry* as "having or inventing something in which one trusts in place of or alongside of the only true God, who has revealed himself in his Word" (Q & A 95).

   Back in 1961 *Christianity Today* reported the answers of a number of theologians and church leaders to the question "What are the most prevalent false gods of our time?" Among many interesting replies, that of the late W. Harry Jellema stood out. He knew the catechism well, and he identified "idolatrous reverence for the self in its solitary and hopeless subjectivity" as the most prevalent false god of his time. He went on to say this: "Two major modes of narcissistic worship then present themselves: either indulgence of the naturalistic drives toward temporal security, power, or pleasure; or the more sophisticated indulgence in the pathos of the self's aloneness and inability to find life worth living."

   Discuss Dr. Jellema's answer. How would the catechism's permission to live in the costly comfort of the first commandment contrast to the way Dr. Jellema described the life of idolatry?

   How would you answer today the question that *Christianity Today* asked back in 1961? How does the catechism liberate us from the idolatry you see around you today?

3. Do you agree that God permits us to live quite secular lives as sacred? Aren't secular and sacred different things? What sense, if any, does the statement make? Why does the author say God permits us to live quite secular lives? And why does he then say God permits us to live these secular lives as sacred?

4. Like Israel who took the ark into battle in hopes of guaranteeing a victory, we may be tempted sometimes to use God rather than to serve him. How? What social effects does this image-making have? How can we avoid seeking to manipulate God?

5. What kinds of blasphemy are there? What sorts do we commit? To what sorts are we "silent bystanders" (Q & A 99)? How, if at all, would an intention to "hallow God's name" affect our social and political and economic intentions?

6. In what sense, if any, are the sabbath laws "social legislation"? How should that affect what we do or don't do on the sabbath? How should it affect our priorities in terms of trying to maintain and nurture honoring the Lord's day in our communities?

Read Leviticus 25. What was the year of jubilee trying to accomplish or preserve? Is that still a good idea? If so, how might it be implemented in today's quite different world?

9

GRATITUDE AND GOD'S PERMISSIONS AGAIN

Q. What is God's will for us
   in the tenth commandment?

A. That not even the slightest thought or desire
      contrary to any one of God's commandments
      should ever arise in my heart.

   Rather, with all my heart
      I should always hate sin
      and take pleasure in whatever is right.

   —*Heidelberg Catechism Q & A 113*

Owe no one anything, except to love one another; for he who loves his neighbor has fulfilled the law. The commandments, "You shall not commit adultery, You shall not kill, You shall not steal, You shall not covet," and any other commandment, are summed up in this sentence, "You shall love your neighbor as yourself." Love does no wrong to a neighbor; therefore love is the fulfilling of the law.

—*Romans 13:8–10*

Here, therefore, let us stand fast: our life shall best conform to God's will and the prescription of the law when it is in every respect most fruitful for our brethren.

—*John Calvin,* Institutes, 2, viii, 54

What God expects of ordinary people is obedience born of gratitude; what God gives ordinary people is forgiveness born of grace. Once forgiven, we hear his commands, not as a burden, but as an invitation to enjoy our humanity, and in our joy to glorify our Creator.

—*Lewis Smedes,* Mere Morality

THE LAW IS THE SHAPE of God's permission to live a new life of gratitude and praise. The "first table" focuses on "what our relation to God should be" (Q & A 93). But, as we discovered in the previous chapter, that relation drives toward concrete expression among our neighbors, politically and economically. The "second table," to which we now turn, focuses "on what we owe our neighbor" (Q & A 93). But it will drive us back again and again to the foundation of God's grace and calling.

The Fifth Permission

Q. What is God's will for us
in the fifth commandment?
A. That I honor, love, and be loyal to
my father and mother
and all those in authority over me;
that I obey and submit to them, as is proper,
when they correct and punish me;
and also that I be patient with their failings—
for through them God chooses to rule us.

—*Heidelberg Catechism Q & A 104*

Abraham Kuyper's little book of meditations on family life, *When Thou Sittest in Thy House*, begins with the words, "The family is that wonderful creation of God from which all our human social life has of itself unfolded." Quite a different kind of book, William Golding's *Lord of the Flies*, makes essentially the same point: the absence of parental influence causes barbarism. Hardly anyone denies the importance of families.

In Aldous Huxley's *Brave New World* Bernard, the rebel against the accepted norms of that totalitarian utopia, was born of a woman who actually used her own womb rather than following the lawfully prescribed test-tube procedures of the London Hatchery and Conditioning Center. Bernard had a story, a history, a family, which gave him identity and character and preserved him from losing his self in the reigning ideology of that brave new day.

Bernard's case is an interesting one to consider in the light of Q & A 104. After all, he could not "honor" both his "deviant" mother and "those in authority" in the "brave new world." He had to choose. He made the right choice, to be sure, but not because parental authority overrides political authority, not because he owed absolute loyalty to his mother rather than to the state. The first table of God's permissions has made it magnificently clear that Bernard owed absolute loyalty only to God. The radical monotheism of the catechism rejects the totalitarian claims of those in authority in the "brave new world" and so justifies Bernard's dissent and disobedience. But it also refuses to permit parents absolute authority over their children. The authority of both parents and government is under God; both are stripped of their claims to absolute rule.

It is totalitarianism of both the fascist and the communist variety—not the catechism—which makes the state a first and absolute value. It is Confucianism, not the catechism, which makes "Honor your parents" a first and absolute principle. The early church, after all, was seen as a threat to Jewish and Roman families—and little wonder, considering the Lord said things like, "I have come to set a man against his father, and a daughter against her mother" (Matt. 10:35; see also Mark 3:31–35). The first crisis of the family was Christianity.

Today, of course, much is said about a new crisis in the family, and Christianity (or at least some religion) is sometimes suggested as a means to preserve and promote family. That suggestion, which sounds laudable, is actually quite misleading. The family that prays together may stay together, but when we use prayer or other religious acts to serve the family, we are in danger of using God instead of serving him.

The family can be—and is to be—enlisted in the cause of God; but God may not be drafted in the cause of the family. Indeed, all authority can be—and is to be—enlisted in the cause of God; but God may not be conscripted in the cause of any authority or government. The catechism places the first table first, and that arrangement is crucial.

When we use God to serve the cause of the family, we're allowing culture's view of the family to remain in control. Perhaps that would not be so bad if our culture had clear and manageable expectations for the family. But it doesn't; as a culture we are confused about the family and confused about the role of parent.

There was a time—and it still is that time in many parts of the world—when the family had a clear economic function. It was an agricultural unit. Now children are an economic liability, not an economic boon.

There was a time—and it still is that time in many parts of the world—when the family had important educational and medical functions as well. But now these are taken care of largely by institutions and persons outside the family.

The nuclear family has emerged as a private refuge of intimacy and care in an industrialized and depersonalized world, and the parent has become the person responsible for coordinating and choosing the experts who really raise the child. It is not surprising, then, that more married couples than ever before are choosing to remain childless, and for a variety

119

of reasons. Some see having children as too great a financial liability, as interfering with the financial security and monetary quest for happiness. Others see having children as a promise of great happiness, but just too much responsibility.

At the same time our culture has extravagant expectations of the "happiness" possible in and from a family and an extravagant sense of the responsibility of parents to produce perfect children. And so the crisis in the family deepens even as religion is used to serve it. For, when the extravagant expectations of happiness are not met, the frustration only increases divorce, abuse, and unfaithfulness. And the awesome responsibility of making perfect children and making children perfect will only lead to the abortion of those fetuses that do not meet our standards and to the neglect of those newborns who are unable to achieve our ideal of the good life or to provide us the happiness we long for and expect from children.

That's why it's important that we recognize that the first table of the law is first. It helps us see that the family can be and is to be enlisted in the cause of God, permitted to serve God, freed from the presumption of its extravagant expectations and responsibilities, freed to be genuinely "under God." Parents and government and all authority are given and called by God. "Through them God chooses to rule us" (Q & A 104). They have a vocation, and that vocation is their legitimate authority.

Parents are called to something quite different than the "happiness" of their children. They are called to give God the glory and to love their neighbor. The child dares to put the question to his parent (Deut. 32:7), and under God the parent is response-able to the child. The parent gives account of his life to the child: the father instructs his son about what is true and good about human existence; the mother directs her daughter's attention to the stories out of which and toward which human life is properly lived.

Imagine a harvest day long ago and a Jewish father out in the field with his observant son. Remember that the Israelite was not to harvest to the very edge of his land. He was not to remove all the grapes from the vine or all fruit from the trees. He was to leave some for the widows and orphans and strangers. The son sees whether his father obeys these commands. He notices whether his father leaves a span (9 inches) or a reed (9 feet); he sees whether his father removes the best fruit and leaves the rest. He sees whether his father honors God and loves his neighbor even in harvesting grain or picking fruit. The child will learn soon enough either to seek first his own welfare or to receive God's permission to honor him and love the neighbor.

There in the field the boy asks, "What do these statutes and judgments mean?" and the father replies, "The Lord brought us out of Egypt with a mighty hand" (cf. Deut. 6:20, 21). That's part of the way God uses families to shape the moral and social sensitivity of the young. The family is God's gift from which all our social life unfolds. The parent's willingness to receive the permission of God to live to his glory and the neighbor's benefit and to initiate his children into a life of faith and faithfulness is the context for the appropriate honor, love, and loyalty due to parents. No parent who makes the sort of reply that Jewish farmer made will be tempted to think "happiness" is what it's all about or to suppose that the perfection that is beyond the parent will be within the reach of the child's obedience (cf. Q & A 114). The family is enlisted in the cause of God, not God in the cause of the family.

The family's vocation is not merely grace at meals. It is surely that, but if it becomes merely that, it quickly degenerates into a graven image or taking God's name in vain. And children know graven images when they see them.

The family's vocation is not merely to provide a context of acceptance and intimacy—insulation against the harsh and demanding world and its "experts." It is surely that, too, but if it becomes merely that, it quickly degenerates into another form of egotism.

The family's vocation is to celebrate God's grace—when we gather around the table and share devotions and laughter and conversation; when the little one takes her first step or spills her first milk; when the eldest talks with Mom about her work and listens to Dad talk with the neighbors or about the neighbors. And all along the way the celebration of God's grace ought to develop the dispositions of neighbor-love and social justice.

Then, like Bernard in *Brave New World*, our children may have a story, a history, and a family which give them identity and character and preserve them from the reigning ideologies of this brave new world. That's the way "God chooses to rule us." To "honor, love, and be loyal" to these parents, these earthen vessels, is permitted, and that alone is permitted. And because they are earthen vessels, children must "be patient with their failings" (Q & A 104). Parents, in a world like this one, after all, are no more likely to be perfect than children.

Neither our children nor our families are "the hope of the future." The catechism will have no truck with such idolatry. Rather, having children is a gesture in the midst of the difficulties and ambiguities of modern life that our hope is in God, and raising children is a vocation to pass that hope on.

The fifth commandment is applied to "all those in authority over me." God chooses to rule us through government too. And government, also, can be and is to be enlisted in the cause of God. Government's vocation is something other than the "happiness" of its citizens or the "law and order" which is blind to injustice and does not care about or for the poor in the land. The government is called to justice. Its legitimate authority depends on that vocation. Governments are permitted to be "God's servant" (Rom. 13:4) to protect us and our neighbors.

The vocation of government is not merely to include "God" in the pledge of allegiance, though we may be glad it's there. It is to institutionalize justice. The vocation of government is not merely to open Senate sessions with prayer, although Peter Marshall's are beautiful. It is, to quote one of Marshall's prayers, "that not only the strong are heard, but also the weak; not only the powerful, but also the helpless; not only those with influence, but also those who have nothing but a case and an appeal." The vocation of government is not merely to stamp "in God we trust" on our coins but also to stamp it on our economic policy. Then to honor, love, and be loyal to these earthen vessels, too, is permitted, and that alone is permitted. And because they are earthen vessels, citizens must "be patient with their failings."

The fifth commandment cannot be heard without at once hearing its vocation to parents and governments and all authority. It does not give them arbitrary dominance; it calls them to legitimate authority. And it calls us to honor God's intention in our parents and in our government. We are to celebrate his presence in their discipline and love, in their refusal to give us what we "want," in their demands that we respect and honor our neighbors, in their legitimate claims upon our obedience.

We should note, finally, that the biblical commandment was not addressed to small children. It was addressed to adults. In our nuclear families, in which only parents and children live together, we usually suppose that the commandment was meant for children and young people. But the normal family structure in Israel was the clan that dwelt together on the inherited land (of which the promise speaks). The aged parents lived on this land with their adult children and their children's children. In this situation the original commandment takes on new meaning. God was telling adult children not to neglect or treat harshly their aged parents, men and women who could no longer work the land. God was reminding adult children that their parents could still tell the stories of their parents and of their parents' parents; they still provided the link to God's covenant in the past; and it was still in relation to them that one had and was true to one's identity.

The original point of the command was respect and protection and care for the aged. That must also be our social concern today. And if the life of the clan is no longer an option, we—as families and churches and a society—must find and sustain other ways to institutionalize and promote respect for the aged.

The Sixth Permission

Q. *What is God's will for us*
  in the sixth commandment?
A. *I am not to belittle, insult, hate, or kill my neighbor—*
    not by my thoughts, my words, my look or gesture,
      and certainly not by actual deeds—
    and I am not to be party to this in others;
    rather, I am to put away all desire for revenge.

I am not to harm or recklessly endanger myself either.

Prevention of murder is also why
  government is armed with the sword.
                    —*Heidelberg Catechism Q & A 105*

Q. Does this commandment refer only to killing?
A. By forbidding murder God teaches us
    that he hates the root of murder:
    envy, hatred, anger, vindictiveness.

In God's sight all such are murder.
                    —*Heidelberg Catechism Q & A 106*

Q. Is it enough then
  that we do not kill our neighbor
  in any such way?
A. No.
  By condemning envy, hatred, and anger
  God tells us
    to love our neighbor as ourselves,
    to be patient, peace-loving, gentle,
      merciful, and friendly to him,
    to protect him from harm as much as we can,
    and to do good even to our enemies.
                    —*Heidelberg Catechism Q & A 107*

When the sixth commandment is set in the context of the first table and of our participation in Christ's righteousness, it does more than prohibit murder. It permits us "to love our neighbor as ourselves, to be patient, peace-loving, gentle, merciful, and friendly to him, to protect him from harm as much as we can, and to do good even to our enemies" (Q & A 107). That is what God permits, and he permits nothing less. It is as Calvin said: "We are accordingly commanded, if we find anything of use to us in saving our neighbors' lives, faithfully to employ it; if there is anything that makes for their peace, to see to it; if anything harmful, to ward it off; if they are in any danger, to lend a helping hand" (2, viii, 39). God permits us to love our neighbor, and the catechism echoes the stringent and heroic morality of the Sermon on the Mount.

But the catechism remains quite realistic about people and about the human tendency to hate. It suggests that seeking justice, taking political responsibility seriously, is part of neighbor love in a world of selfishness. So, says the catechism, "Prevention of murder is also why government is armed with the sword" (Q & A 105). Here the catechism echoes Romans 13:1–7. Justice is not love, but it is a necessary instrument of love in a world of selfishness. Justice restrains selfishness and aggressiveness and so protects our neighbor from violence and harm.

The catechism's politics stand in vivid contrast to the assumptions of many in our culture. The accepted and conventional political motive is to protect and preserve one's own interests. But the catechism calls us, in politics as in all other areas, to look out for the interests of the poor and powerless. Conventional political wisdom acquieses in injustice when by doing so power itself can be preserved. Power, after all, is a tempting idol, and religion is sometimes quite useful in the service of power. But the catechism puts the first table first; God has won the struggle with the gods. He has freed us to see power in its secular reality. We are not permitted to worship it as though it were divine nor flee from it as though it were demonic; we are permitted to give it its legitimate secular status and to use it to honor God and help our neighbor.

Protecting our neighbor requires concerted political action. The implication is not, I think, a Christian political party, but rather an active presence in the arena of political decision—and not just as prophets (even if surely as prophets).

But political responsibility is not the only social implication of the catechism. God's permission to love our neighbor reaches down to politics and to the minimal but adamant claims of justice, but it will not permit the fruit of the Spirit—"love, joy, peace, patience, kindness, goodness, faithfulness, gentleness, self-control" (Gal. 5:22–23, cf. Q & A 107)—to be reduced to the minimal requirements of justice. If we merely work on the purity of our motives and suppress every sign of hostility toward our neighbors (as long as they remain relatively decent toward us and keep up their property), we have not learned to live the catechism. On the other hand, if we allow legal and political issues to monopolize our attention, we have not yet learned to live the catechism either.

God's permission to love our neighbor permits us to work on all the institutions and roles which protect (and sometimes threaten) our neighbor. God's permission to love our neighbor permits us to articulate and to live our fundamental convictions about human life even when they may not be legally enforceable. Only so, perhaps, can we remind our culture that morality is not to be confused with legality nor reduced to it. That reminder would be no small contribution to our society.

The catechism's treatment of the sixth permission, with its concern for the neighbor and its respect for human life, is relevant, of course, to a number of social issues. The pro-life permission of God bears on questions of war, capital punishment, euthanasia, and abortion. Nothing like an adequate treatment of any of these issues can be given in a few pages. Here I would simply make three general comments about these issues and then deal with abortion more concretely.

First, a church that confesses the catechism may and must have these social issues, and the meaning of political responsibility with respect to them, on its agenda as a community of moral discourse and discernment.

Second, the catechism and the Reformed tradition do not make human physical life an absolute value or a first principle. Only God is of absolute value. Only God commands our absolute loyalty. The martyrs understood that well enough. Nevertheless, we must receive human physical life as God's gift. It is valuable; and all those who would honor its giver must protect it. So the burden of proof is always on those who would allow it to go unprotected.

The difficulty of discerning whether and how that burden of proof is borne in particular circumstances of war, capital punishment, abortion, and euthanasia creates some of the most perplexing practical moral problems Christians face in society. The "just war" tradition is one attempt to be faithful to God's pro-life permission within the ambiguities and realities of our world and our history. I think we need a formally similar approach to the issues of capital punishment, euthanasia, and abortion.

Third, and this much is certain: the catechism's pro-life stance will not permit the crusader mentality in war, vindictiveness in punishment, the disposition to look hospitably on the death of the weak and "defective," and the abortionist mentality, which treats the taking of life as though it needs no justification.

In 1972 the church of which I am a member put the pro-life permission of the commandment and of the catechism in very strong terms in a ruling on abortion. It held that unless an abortion was performed to save the life of the mother, this procedure is prohibited by the sixth commandment. Less than a year later, the Supreme Court of the United States ruled in *Roe* v. *Wade* that state laws prohibiting abortion before a fetus is viable were unconstitutional. The court held that decisions about abortion were fundamentally private decisions, to be made in the context of conversations between a woman and her physician.

Partisans in the abortion debate have felt obliged to praise or deride *Roe* v. *Wade*. The decision is still celebrated by advocates of a woman's right to abort and still scorned by advocates of a fetus's right to life. I would not defend *Roe* v. *Wade* as a model of legal reasoning and I hasten to say that the outcome of that decision has been a callous and frightening disregard for fetal life and welfare. But I do think that opponents to the outcome of *Roe* v. *Wade* may learn a lesson or two from that decision, lessons that are important if we would live consistently in the pro-life permission of the catechism. As I see it, *Roe* v. *Wade* can remind us that the most important social opposition to the outcome of its holdings may be moral and professional, not legal.

Roe v. *Wade* recognized that the moral status of the fetus was disputable, and the court did not pretend to be wise enough to decide this issue. A frequent criticism of the reasoning of the court is precisely that, although it claimed to be unable to resolve this "difficult" question, for all practical purposes it did implicitly decide it: since the *Roe* v. *Wade* decision, the fetus is not protected by law until viable. But the court, it must be noted,

125

held only that the legal status of the fetus may be distinguished from the moral status of the fetus and that there was no precedent for holding that the fetus has a legal status that entitles it to the same protection of the law extended to persons.

This is the first point we must see—not that the legal ruling of *Roe* v. *Wade* was right, but that *Roe* v. *Wade* quite clearly distinguished legal questions from moral questions. That its legal holding was taken as moral license is a reflection on our society rather than on the court. Opponents to the outcome of *Roe* v. *Wade* who focus their energy exclusively on statutes like Helms' "human life statute" or on constitutional amendments like Hatch's "federalist" human life amendment do not fundamentally address our society's reduction of morality to legality.

It is as a friend of mine, Helen John, once said, "It's not enough to outlaw abortion; you have to outlove it." That suggests a "more excellent way" to oppose the outcome of *Roe* v. *Wade*, a way that follows the cue of *Roe* v. *Wade* itself, distinguishing legal questions from moral questions. Feminist that she is, Sister Helen has reminded me that men tend to take abortion lightly, whether in opposing it or in supporting it. We tend to make it an issue of "rights" of individuals, so that the only important question becomes whether the fetus is an individual or not. Sister Helen insists she has not known a woman contemplating abortion to treat the issue quite like that—as though she were exercising simple ownership rights over her own body, like a landlady with an undesirable tenant or pest. She insists that women experience and understand the genuine tragedy of abortion, the bitterly hard choice under fearful pressure which ends with a rifled and bleeding womb and shreds of crimson life. She insists that women understand abortion as violence, as a desperate violence inflicted by a woman not only upon an embryo but also upon herself.

To outlaw abortion, then, will not remove the desperate necessity of abortion for some women or the tragic character of the lives of some women. Respect for life among Christians must be joined with an effective support system—including financial, psychological, medical, social, and moral support—for women and their children. These must be joined in the moral life of our communities and in our political rhetoric and action.

"It's not enough to outlaw abortion; you have to outlove it." Sister Helen suggested this point may have been made before: "Woe to you lawyers also! for you load men with burdens hard to bear, and you yourselves do not touch the burdens with one of your fingers" (Luke 11:46).

Roe v. *Wade* distinguished the moral status of the fetus from the legal status of the fetus. The moral question is, as Stan Hauerwas has said, not so much a question of "When does life begin?" but of "Who is life's true sovereign?" Opponents to the outcome of *Roe* v. *Wade* have argued desperately that the legal status of the fetus ought to be guaranteed because of genetic uniqueness and completeness, or because of individualization, or because of potentiality, or because of electrical activity in the brain of an eight-week old fetus, or. . . . Such arguments are abstract, interminable, divisive, frustrating, and futile. Taking their cue from *Roe* v. *Wade*, Christians should begin to reflect upon and to tell their own reasons for ascribing a certain moral status to the fetus, regardless of its legal status. For Christians, the moral status of the fetus is tied not to genetic uniqueness and completeness but to the sovereign grace of God. The question to which we should direct attention is not "When does life really begin?" but "Whom shall we trust?" and "In whom shall we hope?"

God reigns, even over a world marked and marred by tragedy; and therefore life, even the prenatal beginnings of it, may be received as a gift from God's gracious and nurturing hand. God will reign, and his cosmic sovereignty will have no challenge. Therefore Christians sign and seal their trust in God's future by having and loving children, by refusing to consign or abandon any developing life to the realm or powers of darkness. In the midst of tragedy, Christians hope. Because they hope, they may welcome, protect, and nurture children. Because they acknowledge tragedy, they may acknowledge as well that sometimes abortion may mournfully, repentantly, tearfully, be indicated.

This sort of argument can hardly be articulated in the courts or legislatures of our land. That doesn't mean we should refrain from articulating legal arguments. The legal issues are thorny and nettling, but they will not go away. The point is rather that we, taking a cue from *Roe* v. *Wade*, should not allow our attention to be monopolized by the legal issues; we should not refrain from articulating our fundamental convictions about human life, even though they may not be legally enforceable. If we do renege on this opportunity to witness to our convictions, as I fear we have, then we abandon our society to its own conceptions of morality as legality.

Finally, in *Roe* v. *Wade* the court wanted to leave the moral controversy about the status of the fetus within that private arena of conversation between a woman and her doctor. The court presumed that the question of abortion would be a "medical decision" and that the professional ethic of physicians would act to restrict abortion even if were legalized. *Roe* v. *Wade* quite clearly relied on a vital professional integrity among physicians to restrict what it held the law could not prohibit. "Basic responsibility for the abortion decision must rest with the physician." That the court's legal ruling was taken by many physicians as an entrepreneurial opportunity is reason to judge the profession rather than the ruling.

The cue here from *Roe* v. *Wade* for those who oppose the outcome of this trial is the importance of nurturing a professional ethic among physicians; of attending to the vows, oaths, stories, and traditions that have formed and informed the art of medicine and the character of physicians; of resisting the tendency to reduce professions to skills learned by technical training and accessible to consumers.

Those who oppose what has happened since *Roe* v. *Wade* must insist that physicians refuse to participate in actions that violate their professional integrity or serve ends alien to the practice of medicine. They must help hospitals articulate professional policy that sets limits on justifiable abortion and then represents such limits in conversation with a pregnant woman.

The *Roe* v. *Wade* decision is now a decade old. During these past ten years medicine has almost lost the opportunity to reassert itself as a practice, different from the practices of law or the marketplace. But the cue from *Roe* v. *Wade* is that the attempt to do so is both possible and worthwhile. During the past ten years the church has almost lost the opportunity to express its own profoundest convictions about why fetuses and embryos and zygotes are to be welcomed and cherished, convictions different in kind from arguments about when life begins legitimately to claim legal protection. But the cue from Roe v. Wade is that the attempt is both possible and worthwhile. During these past ten years society has almost lost the opportunity to demonstrate its support of women and children in the midst of the tragedy and the desperation that make abortion look like an option. But the cue from *Roe* v. *Wade* is that the attempt to do so is both possible and worthwhile. The outcome of *Roe* v. *Wade* is morally horrifying, but those opposed to that outcome might have learned—and might still learn, ten years later—some important lessons from that decision.

The Seventh Permission

*Q. What is God's will for us
in the seventh commandment?*
*A. God condemns all unchastity.
We should therefore thoroughly detest it
and, married or single,
live decent and chaste lives.*
—Heidelberg Catechism Q & A 108

*Q. Does God, in this commandment,
forbid only such scandalous sins as adultery?*
*A. We are temples of the Holy Spirit, body and soul,
and God wants both to be kept clean and holy.
That is why he forbids
everything which incites unchastity,
whether it be actions, looks, talk, thoughts, or desires.*
—Heidelberg Catechism Q & A 109

The seventh commandment and the catechism's interpretation of it existed long before the pill, *Playboy*, and pornographic films. Some claim that the ancient wisdom has become folly, that we have finally broken through puritan prudery to a sexual renaissance. There is no doubt, I guess, that we are living in a sexual revolution in which many traditional mores are being challenged and upset. But that sexual revolution sometimes looks very much like a sexual wilderness or a demonic transformation of God's good gift.

This social revolution challenges those who confess the catechism not only to present their sexuality to God but also to point the way through the sexual wilderness for others, to witness to God's intentions with sexuality. It challenges us to speak openly and candidly and Christianly about sex.

"God condemns all unchastity" (Q & A 108); "he forbids everything which incites unchastity" (Q & A 109). It is tempting merely to repeat those words to our culture—and to our young people. And many give in to that temptation. I remember sermons that used the catechism as a whip to get the young people to behave themselves. I also remember how exciting and adventuresome such sermons made unchastity sound and how boring "righteousness" seemed.

The catechism, we must not forget, puts the law in the context of God's grace. It points us to the grace of God enabling and permitting us to live genuinely human and faithful lives. We misuse the catechism if we use it merely to judge and condemn, merely to congratulate ourselves on our righteousness or flagellate ourselves for our weakness. The seventh commandment is God's permission to live our lives, including our sexual lives, as God gives and claims them. We may even discover (before it's too late) that the adventuresome and heroic life is in chastity; that unchastity, however titillating it may be, is finally boring and usually messy.

The catechism condemns unchastity because it values human persons—or, rather, because God values human persons. He made us, body and soul, with the power to make and keep covenant. "We are temples of the Holy Spirit, body and soul" (Q & A 109). If we miss that affirmation, we miss the catechism's permission to live our sexual lives as God gives and claims them. That, of course, is all the catechism will permit, and so it condemns unchastity. But the catechism does not disapprove of the body or of our sexuality, does not disparage or devalue it, does not treat it as something dirty and dismal and dingy. Bodies are not prison-houses for souls; they are temples of the Holy Spirit.

The catechism knows that sex is not a bowl of buttons. Many Sunday afternoons ago, when I was a boy, I would play with the bowl of buttons my mother kept in her sewing and mending cabinet. I would dump the buttons out and try to flip them back into the bowl. The fun was the technique, and the importance of it for my young hands was skill and dexterity. Sex is not like that; sex is not a bowl of buttons. It is not simply a matter of technique and dexterity, a matter of skill. Sex has meaning beyond the quality of its performance. Yet sex as skill, as performance, as dexterity, as a bowl of buttons, is the vision of sexuality one most frequently sees in our sex-saturated society: the proper technique and presto—fulfillment. As the bumper sticker says, "If it feels good, do it."

The catechism knows there is something as mysterious about sex as there is about persons and about temples. No matter how much we know about technique, sex remains a mystery. This is the mystery: that two persons become one flesh (Gen.2:24, 1 Cor. 6:15–20). Sexual relations always involve us as whole persons, body and soul, with our capacity to make and keep covenant. It is God's permission that we live our sexual lives not merely as technical experts but as whole persons, not merely as pleasure-seekers but as convenant-makers and covenant-keepers.

There remains, I suppose, in every act of coitus a sign of God's permission to live our sexual lives as he gives and claims them, for there remains an implicit exchange of commitments. To ask during the intimacies of making love, "But will you love me tomorrow?" is to impugn the committal of the act. Something in the sexual act itself escapes any tendency to reduce sex to a technology of pleasure and pain and reminds us of God's permission to live our sexual lives as he gives and claims them. Of this I am sure: our confrontation with our own sexuality calls us to make important decisions not only about the meaning of sex—whether a technology of pleasure or a mystery of commitment—but also about ourselves—whether we are pleasure-seekers and self-fulfillers or covenant-makers and covenant-keepers.

We may—and we should—delight in this mystery. Witness the Song of Solomon. And we should—and we may—be sober about this mystery. Witness Proverbs 7. The sexual act celebrates the mystery of one whole and exclusive relationship covenanted between two persons who are committed not only to each other but also to the cause of the one who creates and keeps covenant and renews all things, including them. The sexual act celebrates not the act itself, not technique, not even the intensity of attraction two people can feel for each other or the fulfillment of desire one person can find in another. It celebrates a covenant, begun in vows, carried out in fidelity, and given to a future of Christ's righteousness, Christ's service, also and especially, toward each other.

Such is the delight and sobriety of sex in marriage. Such is the gift and claim of God. And it is because God permits us such a sexual life that he refuses to permit us to treat sexuality without mystery, without delight, or without sobriety; that he "forbids everything which incites unchastity" (Q & A 109). Such sobriety continues to be part of the Christian view of sexuality. It is not prudish, but sober. It commends delight, but ties it to the mystery. It does not even condemn technique or pleasure or the fulfillment of each in the other, but it subordinates these to the mystery, delight, and sobriety of the covenant-making and covenant-keeping of a man and a woman in the Lord. Technique, after all, may enhance the intensity of delight for a moment, but technique alone quickly becomes boring (witness the bowl of buttons), and sexual relations reduced to technique for pleasure quickly move from one technique to other more exotic ones. Commitment and covenant provide less intensity, to be sure, but more continuity; and sexual relations within covenant can slowly advance to the consummate pleasure of holding hands in memory and promise.

The church that hears the catechism's permission to live chaste lives as part of the adventure of convenant might be a voice calling in our sexual wilderness, calling married or single to a heroic life in the quest for and promise of Christ's righteousness, preparing the way of the Lord. The church has a vocation to speak openly, candidly, Christianly, and publicly about sex.

The church's public voice about sex must remain fundamentally positive. Censorship is a dangerous option not only because of some questions about the legitimate use of power but also because it risks allowing God's permission to be mistaken for prudery. There are other options, more positive ones: We may witness to God's permission by subsidizing positive statements of the Christian understanding of sex in art and literature. We may be concerned about sex education, providing programs that alert young people not only to physiology and technique but also to mystery, and which nurture the responses of delight and sobriety within an adventure of convenant. In all of this we may be confident that the next generation's attitude toward sex will be formed and informed not only by television producers or social engineers or sexual researchers but also and fundamentally by the dispositions and attitudes and actions of ordinary men and women shaped by the gift and claim of God.

The Eighth Permission

Q. What does God forbid
in the eighth commandment?
A. He forbids not only outright theft and robbery,
punishable by law.

But in God's sight theft also includes
cheating and swindling our neighbor
by schemes made to appear legitimate,
such as:
inaccurate measurements of weight, size, or volume;
fraudulent merchandising;
counterfeit money;
excessive intrest;
or any other means forbidden by God.

In addition he forbids all greed
and pointless squandering of his gifts.

—*Heidelberg Catechism Q & A 110*

Q. What does God require of you
   in this commandment?
A. That I do whatever I can
   for my neighbor's good,
   that I treat him
     as I would like others to treat me,
   and that I work faithfully
     so that I may share with those in need.

                    —Heidelberg Catechism Q & A 111

"Thou shalt not steal," the commandment says, but the catechism knows there are many kinds of theft. It acknowledges that the command forbids theft by violence, but it seems little interested in that. Like the Scriptures, the catechism emphasizes thefts by deceit and advantage (Q & A 110).

The prophet Amos, that peasant shepherd from Tekoa, the tender of sycamore trees, spoke God's word of judgment against Israel "because they sell the righteous for silver, and the needy for a pair of shoes—they that trample the head of the poor into the dust of the earth, and turn aside the way of the afflicted" (2:6,7). Those were "good times" in Israel. Jeroboam II had restored the fortunes of Israel. The nation was at a new zenith politically and economically. But the rich only grew richer while the poor grew poorer. And Amos condemned those who "make the ephah small and the shekel great, and deal deceitfully with false balances . . . and sell the refuse of the wheat" (8:5–6).

Amos, like the writers of the catechism, knew that there are many kinds of theft. Theft always takes some kind of power. The only power accessible to the poor is violence. The rich have subtler kinds of power to steal with: the measures and the merchandising and lending. But "in God's sight" all such use of power against a neighbor for one's own advantage is theft.

We need not pause too long over these different kinds of stealing, but we may at least observe that some social intentions are implicit here. The person or the church that confesses the catechism is pledged to protect the consumer from fraud and deceit. And the special object of such protection is not ourselves but the poor and powerless.

"In addition," the catechism says, "he forbids all greed" (Q & A 110). Again the command is really a permission. God's grace permits and enables us to live the new life—also economically—and that is all he permits. He forbids greed because he permits us to live in his grace and for his glory also in the economic dimensions of our life.

The catechism permits us to be thrifty even as it forbids waste, "the pointless squandering of his gifts" (Q & A 110). But it's important to remember that greed is sometimes subtly disguised as "honest thrift."

That's how, I suppose, the rich farmer who built barns to store all his grain and his goods (Luke 12:15–21, referred to in Q & A 110) would have disguised his actions and intentions. As a matter of fact, nothing in the story suggests that the farmer had made his fortune in any dishonest way or by any of the various kinds of theft. He had apparently acquired his fortune by hard work and practical know-how and the farsighted vision of a good businessman. Yet Jesus called him a "fool". The verdict is rather shocking. If he were alive today, I think fewer of us would call him "fool" than would admire and envy him.

Why then did Jesus call him "fool"? Because he did not see the opportunity of gratitude to God for his deliverance and his gift of the land and its fruit. He did not see the opportunity to rejoice in God's mercy by being generous himself. He did not see God's permission to love God and his neighbors—the sojourner, the fatherless, the widow, the poor. And so he was a "fool". He was not a fool because he was thrifty but because, however he might disguise it, he was greedy, covetous, convinced that life and happiness could be secured by the abundance of his possessions. And so Jesus called him a "fool."

Before we cast too many stones in the direction of the first century, however, perhaps we had better examine ourselves and our society. Greed still says, and says more loudly and demandingly than ever, "More is better; more will secure and guarantee my happiness or the nation's flourishing." But, if Scripture is to be believed, greed is still folly. The Scripture teaches that unrestricted material indulgence is more likely to deaden and corrupt us than to enliven and free us. Wisdom still says, "Enough is best." As the wise man prayed, "Give me neither poverty nor riches; feed me with the food that is needful for me, lest I be full, and deny thee, and say, 'Who is the Lord?' or lest I be poor, and steal, and profane the name of my God" (Prov. 30:8,9). "More is better" is folly; "enough is best" is wisdom. Are our lives lived in folly or in God's grace?

"Enough is best." But it's not always easy to determine how much is "enough." Larry Rasmussen puts it this way:

> The outer boundaries, at least, are clear. Real poverty is not enough. It kills the spirit and debilitates the body. It beats people down before they can walk even half tall. It brutalizes cell and soul alike. An economy that has the resources to meet basic human needs—food, shelter, clothing, health care, work, festivity—and does not meet them, fails the test. And any economy that simultaneously generates debilitating poverty in some quarters and unrestrained consumption in others has failed doubly.

Neither our economy nor we ourselves are free from folly. But the catechism puts such judgment in the context of God's grace. God's righteousness frees us from greed, from the assumptions that "more is better," that "more will provide security and happiness," and that a person's life consists in the abundance of things. God permits us to live simply and as stewards of his gifts. Calvin's remark on stewardship is apropos:

We are the stewards of everything God has conferred on us by which we are able to help our neighbor, and are required to render account of our stewardship. Moreover, the only right stewardship is that which is tested by the rule of love (3, vii, 5).

That's exactly what the catechism goes on to say: "What does God require of you in this commandment? That I do whatever I can for my neighbor's good, that I treat him as I would like others to treat me, and that I work faithfully so that I may share with those in need" (Q & A 111).

What are the social implications of loving our neighbor in the economy? What would an economic system look like if we had the courage of comfort? The implications are legion. It is easier, of course, to *state* economic goals that are implications of loving our neighbor in the economy than it is to find the complex means to achieve these goals. In employment, loving each neighbor suggests trying to secure a job for everyone who is able to hold a job and seeking employment. In housing, developing a system that treats each one as I would be treated means striving for decent housing for all. In health care, doing whatever I can for my neighbor's good means working toward adequate health care for all. We could continue to list goals—in education, income, justice, recreation, and so on. We could also develop some of the further implications of each of these. The goal of full employment, for example, demands the more immediate goal of ending racially restrictive practices in unions, in apprenticeship programs, and in membership procedures.

To state all the economic goals that are entailed by the catechism's permission to "do whatever I can for my neighbor's good" and to formulate realistic means for their accomplishment are far beyond the scope of this little book and far beyond the reach of my competence. They will take the continuing moral discourse of the church that confesses the catechism. They will demand the contributions and gifts of economists and laborers, of moralists and mothers, of employers and managers. I lack, you see, not only the time and space for such a project but also many of the required gifts.

In all our discussions we must continue to recognize that the catechism calls us to love our neighbor in the world of the economy. It calls us to new economic dispositions and new economic structures. What those are and how they can be formed must be a matter of communal prayer and discernment in churches that confess the catechism. It is not enough simply to refrain from violent theft. It is not enough simply to refrain from using our power to cheat the poor. It is not enough even to purge our greed. God gives and claims our stewardship. God enables and requires us to love and help our neighbor, also in the economy. God permits us to learn and then to do what that requires, and he permits nothing else.

The Ninth Permission

Q. What is God's will for us
in the ninth commandment?
A. God's will is that I
never give false testimony against anyone,
twist no one's words,
not gossip or slander,
nor join in condemning anyone
without a hearing or without a just cause.

Rather, in court and everywhere else,
I should avoid lying and deceit of every kind;
these are devices the devil himself uses,
and they would call down on me God's intense anger.
I should love the truth,
speak it candidly,
and openly acknowledge it.
And I should do what I can
to guard and advance my neighbor's good name.
—Heidelberg Catechism Q & A 112

An announcement made by former President Nixon's press secretary—that all the president's earlier statements were "inoperative"—is often viewed as the climax in the development of of "the credibility gap." People had started talking about such a gap during the Vietnam War. They grew skeptical as they listened, time after time, to assurances from government officials that good progress was being made in the war, that the investment of a little more money and a few more young people would bring the war to a close and end communism's threat in Southeast Asia. As cynicism about the government's statements spread, people became less and less inclined to expect honesty.

The effect of deceit, even for so noble a cause as "to save the presidency," is no less debilitating to a society than to a friendship. Neither society nor friendship can survive without a modicum of integrity. That's why the catechism insists that those who serve God "love the truth, speak it candidly, and openly acknowledge it" (Q & A 112).

Truthfulness is what God permits—and commands. How could it be any other way? God permits us to live in Christ, who is the truth, and in his Spirit of truth. God has fought with sin and death and the devil, who is "the father of lies" (John 8:44), and he has won. To live in his victory and his grace means to love the truth, to demand the truth, to nurture and sustain a public order that can endure the truth.

The ninth commandment was, first of all, a rule against perjury at the Gate, the place where testimony was heard and legal rulings made. The catechism knows that the permission of God to be truthful is relevant to behavior "in court" (Q & A 112). And it's important to note that the implications the catechism draws have to do not only with the prohibition of "false testimony" but also with the protection of due process. We may not and must not "join in condemning anyone without a hearing or without a just cause" (Q & A 112). To confess the catechism should nurture a disposition to protect due process for all our neighbors, even our enemies and alleged criminals.

The state is not the only place where due process is important, of course. In the church we are sometimes far too ready to "join in condemning" the "heretic" among us. It is a mark of confessional integrity when a church adopts and implements a judicial code to protect due process in the church for its members.

The catechism also knows, of course, that God's permission of truthfulness is also relevant "everywhere else" (Q & A 112). In conversations with other people and in conversations about other people, God permits no "gossip or slander." In theological disputes he allows us to "twist no one's words." In government he permits no devices of "lying and deceit." Everywhere we are permitted truthfulness—and only truthfulness.

The catechism's view of truthfulness is not the mere conformity of our words to our thoughts. It finally explicates God's permission in terms of our duty "to guard and advance my neighbor's good name" (Q & A 112). The catechism evidently knows that there is what Augustine calls a murderous truth, what Bonhoeffer calls a satanic truth—a truth-telling that callously sacrifices the welfare and reputation of a neighbor. Human pride and enmity can turn even the truth to evil use by damaging the neighbor. The catechism echoes Calvin here, who condemns the "poisoned sweetness experienced in ferreting out and in disclosing the evils of others" and refuses to excuse such conduct on the basis that "we are not lying" (2, viii, 48). It also echoes Scripture, of course, with its simple and profound instruction to speak the truth in love (Eph. 4:15).

The Tenth Permission

The catechism treats the tenth commandment as a kind of summary of the whole law. Calvin treated it similarly. "The purpose of this commandment is," he said (2, viii, 49), that "since God wills that our whole soul be possessed with a disposition to love, we must banish from our hearts all desire contrary to love."

God liberates us to be totally his. Our comfort is that we are not our own. And, because we are his, "not even the slightest thought or desire contrary to any one of God's commandments should ever arise in [our] heart[s]" (Q & A 113). God permits us to "take pleasure in whatever is right" (Q & A 113). By God's grace we live lives that not only keep God's commandments but also delight in them.

The catechism quickly reminds us, however, that such radical righteousness is no simple possibility in this age. "In this life even the holiest have only a small beginning of this obedience" (Q & A 114). Again, even in the context of the kind of life God gives and enables, the catechism combines the command of love with realism about human sin. The new persons who "begin to live according to all, not only some, of God's commandments" (Q & A 114) continue to be constrained and permitted to seek justice. Love that is realistic about human sin may aim for a good deal more than justice, but it can accept nothing less than justice without becoming something less than love.

Our sanctification in this life, our "striving to be renewed more and more after God's image" (Q & A 115) in this life, must, therefore, surely include the formation of our character, dispositions, and actions to the contours of justice. The law is the shape of our costly comfort in the catechism, and the Christian community is permitted the courage of her comfort in politics and economics, in the family, in the midst of a sexual revolution, in the face of hunger, in short, in "all our living" (Q & A 86).

That renewal after God's image is his promise and his claim. It is no alien obligation. It is God's permission to live our own new humanity. It remains the very law that judges us (Q & A 115), but God has put us on our way to full and new humanity. And that way includes social righteousness.

Acknowledgments and Suggestions for Further Reading

Lewis Smedes's *Mere Morality* (Grand Rapids: Wm. B. Eerdmans, 1983), quoted at the beginning of this chapter (from the book's page 243), is an excellent resource for further reflection about each of the commandments treated in this chapter.

The quotation of Abraham Kuyper is from his *When Thou Sittest in Thy House* (Grand Rapids: Wm. B. Eerdmans, 1929).

I owe the illustration of the child accompanying his father to the field to Lambert Ponstein's privately circulated manuscript on the decalogue, "Learning about Love."

On the family I am especially indebted to Stanley Hauerwas's *A Community of Character* (Notre Dame: University of Notre Dame Press, 1981), pages 155–174, and Smedes's *Mere Morality*, pages 67–98. The quotation of Peter Marshall's prayer is from *Prayers offered by the Chaplain the Rev. Peter Marshall, D.D.: 1947–1949* (Washington: U. S. Government Printing Office, 1949), June 4, 1948.

On the sixth commandment, the works of Hauerwas, *A Community of Character*, pages 196–229, and Smedes, *Mere Morality*, pages 99–156, are especially helpful.

The discussion of *Roe* v. *Wade* is reprinted from Allen Verhey, "Learning from *Roe* v. *Wade*," *The Reformed Journal* (April 1983), pp. 3–5.

The CRC decision on abortion may be found in *Acts of Synod 1972*, pages 63–64. Also see the study committee's report, *ibid.*, pages 479–484.

On the seventh commandment see especially Hauerwas's *A Community of Character*, pages 175–195, and Smedes's *Mere Morality*, pages 157–182.

On the eighth commandment see Smedes's *Mere Morality*, pages 183–210, and Larry Rasmussen's *Economic Anxiety and Christian Faith* (Minneapolis: Augsburg Publishing House, 1981). The quotation is from pages 78–79.

On the ninth commandment see Smedes's *Mere Morality*, pages 211–238. The judicial code may be found in *Acts of Synod 1975*, pages 617–626.

In discussion question 1 you might consult Allen Verhey's "The Test-tube Baby Boom: Technology and Parenting" in *The Banner*, Nov. 14, 1983, p. 8. The case in discussion question 3 is treated in Allen Verhey's "Integrity, Humility, and Heroism" in the *Reformed Journal*, March, 1982, pages 18–21. In discussion question 4, the reference to Hauerwas's law comes from a public lecture at Hope College, Holland, Michigan. The thought experiment in question 5 is indebted to a similar one in Rasmussen's book, pages 75–76, and to John Rawls's *A Theory of Justice* (Cambridge, Mass.: Harvard University Press, 1971).

Discussion Questions for Chapter 9

1. Do you agree that our society is confused about the family today? What evidence have you found that society believes that children are a way of providing happiness for parents or that children are the hope of the future? What evidence have you found that many believe parents are responsible for making their children perfect or happy?

   How might the catechism respond to any of these views of parents and children? How does the catechism's view of the family influence the way our families live?

   Today a whole new technology of giving birth is being developed. What might a community formed by the catechism think about *in vitro* fertilization, for example?

2. Do you agree with Sister Helen John that it's not enough to outlaw abortion, you have to outlove it? What would "outloving abortion" require of a church? Consider, for example, the following case study:

   A local congregation had purchased an old apartment building to use for church education. Before it was renovated for that purpose, however, a Christian adoption agency suggested the building be used to minister to unwed and pregnant teenagers. The agency offered to provide Christian counseling in addition to medical, social, and moral support for pregnant young women—if the church would let them use the building rent-free. But the church still owed a good deal of money on the building and, while not desperately cramped, could have used some more class-rooms.

A proposal to let the agency use the building came to the congregational meeting. One member spoke in support of the proposal, "If we do not provide such support, I do not want to hear another voice from this congregation raised in horror about abortion."

"But," another member said, "the real business of the church is to preach and teach the gospel. We should be using that building for church education, not some social program."

How would you vote? Do you agree with either of the comments made? Explain.

3. The movie *Whose Life Is It, Anyway?* tells the story of a young sculptor who was left a quadriplegic by an automobile accident and kept alive only by regular dialysis treatments.

Although the young man was alert and articulate, he began to question the wisdom of living when his sculptor hands no longer responded to his brain or his world. The doctor who had saved his life prescribed a valium; the patient refused it. The doctor then injected the quadriplegic with valium against his will. That act determined the patient's course. He asserted his legal power to stop the dialysis treatments and to render the doctor powerless to "save" him. The doctor, in turn, began to crusade to have the patient declared "incompetent," to render him finally powerless and without options so that the doctor could protect his life.

Suppose you were the judge called to rule on this case. What would you decide and why?

4. The author contrasts understanding the sexual act as a technology of pleasure and understanding it as commitment and covenant. Is this a valid contrast? Why or why not? In your discussion also consider whether the sex act is "naturally" a matter of commitment or whether we make it such by understanding it that way. By the way, is unchastity or chastity more exciting and adventuresome and heroic? Why?

This talk of commitment and covenant may be a lot for young people to remember alone in the dark with passions stirring. The level of commitment is hard to test in moments like that without self-deception. Perhaps before such moments young people might ask themselves questions to determine the honesty of their commitment, questions like: "Is our love honest if we need to express it secretly?" What other questions might they ask of themselves?

This talk of commitment and covenant may be a lot for married people to remember in a quarrel with angry passions stirring. Hauerwas's law is, "You always marry the wrong person." What do you think this means, and do you agree with Hauerwas? Do we fall in love and then get married, or do we get married and then learn what love means? Does love create a marriage, or does marriage teach us what love requires?

5. An Experiment

The following experiment could be done in groups of four to six persons each. You will need an entire session to complete the task.

You are a group of people who have to create a just economic order from scratch. None of you knows what place you will have in the new society, whether you will be smart or retarded, black or white, male or female, young or old. Your task is to sketch in broad strokes the ways in which you will insure fair distribution of economic burdens and benefits. The new community is small, say 5,000 members, and has adequate but limited material resources.

Among the questions your planning should address are the following: What products and services does the society need? Who will provide them? How will such production and service be rewarded? How will you provide for those who are too young or too old or too disabled to provide for themselves? Who will provide such service? Is caring for them an important service? Should everyone benefit equally from being a member of this society? Or should those who contribute more to the society benefit more? How will you decide who contributes more? Should scarce talents be rewarded more than abundant talents?

Now try to articulate the fundamental moral principles of your economic order, bringing in what you've learned so far from the catechism. Finally, compare your model economy with the economic order you know in real life. What changes are required, either in your model economy or in the real one?

6. Take some time this week to privately reflect on what the catechism says about each of the ten permissions (commandments). For each permission, try to decide on one specific social action which you will undertake (or at least begin to undertake) in order to more fully "live the catechism."

10

PRAYERS FOR A SOCIAL AWAKENING

Q. No one in this life
  can obey the Ten Commandments perfectly:
  Why then does God want them
  preached so pointedly?

A. First, so that the longer we live
    the more we may come to know our sinfulness
    and the more eagerly look to Christ
      for forgiveness of sins and righteousness.

  Second, so that,
    while praying to God for the grace of the Holy Spirit,
  we may never stop striving
    to be renewed more and more after God's image,
  until after this life we reach our goal:
    perfection.

  —Heidelberg Catechism Q & A 115

Q. Why do Christians need to pray?

A. Because prayer is the most important part
    of the thankfulness God requires of us.
  And also because God gives his grace and Holy Spirit
  only to those who pray continually and groan inwardly,
    asking God for these gifts
    and thanking him for them.

  —Heidelberg Catechism Q & A 116

141

Q. How does God want us to pray
  so that he will listen to us?

A. First, we must pray from the heart
    to no other than the one true God,
      who has revealed himself in his Word,
      asking for everything he has commanded us to ask for.

  Second, we must acknowledge our need and misery,
    hiding nothing,
    and humble ourselves in his majestic presence.

  Third, we must rest on this unshakable foundation:
    even though we do not deserve it,
    God will surely listen to our prayer
      because of Christ our Lord.
  That is what he promised us in his Word.
                          —Heidelberg Catechism Q & A 117

Lord, teach us to pray.

                                    —Luke 11:1

You invoke as Father him who judges each one impartially.

                                    —1 Peter 1:17

A mighty fortress is our God,
A bulwark never failing;
Our helper he, amid the flood
of mortal ills prevailing.
For still our ancient foe
Doth seek to work us woe;
His craft and power are great,
And armed with cruel hate,
On earth is not his equal.

Did we in our own strength confide,
Our striving would be losing;
Were not the right Man on our side,
The Man of God's own choosing.
Dost ask who that may be?
Christ Jesus, it is he;
Lord Sabaoth his name,

From age to age the same,
And He must win the battle.
—"A Mighty Fortress Is Our God," Martin Luther.

It remains for us to seek in him, and in prayers to ask of him, what we have
learned to be in him.
—Calvin, Institutes, *3, xx, 1*

The heart of the Christian ethos is that those who are freed and summoned to
pray "Thy kingdom come" are also freed and summoned to use their freedom
to obey the command that is given therewith and to live for their part with a
view to the coming kingdom.
—Karl Barth, The Christian Life

THE CLOSING SECTION of the catechism comments on the
Lord's Prayer. Nowhere is the Heidelberg's reputation for devotional
quality more deserved: each answer is itself a beautiful short prayer. And
nowhere is the catechism's social interest more fittingly expressed: each
beautiful little prayer for the reign of God's grace nurtures certain social
intentions and dispositions.

The catechism turns to prayer after dealing with the law. Acknowledging that even the holiest make only a small beginning in the obedience
God permits and requires, the Heidelberg insists that the commandments,
nevertheless, are to be preached pointedly. Such preaching is important
"so that, while praying to God for the grace of the Holy Spirit, we may never
stop striving to be renewed more and more after God's image" (Q & A 115).

Prayer and "striving to be renewed more and more after God's
image" are inseparable. The intention of prayer is not to get things out of
God but rather to get ourselves formed and reformed by the mind of God
in Jesus Christ. Prayer is thus part of our gratitude (Q & A 116). Prayer does
not evade life with its problems and ambiguities and perplexities; it embraces life—that life which God gives and claims—and asks God for the
grace and power to live it as he permits. Prayer does not negate this world
and this history in some spiritual flight to God; it affirms God's creative
power and providential care in this world and this history and asks God to
establish his cosmic reign against the powers of evil and injustice which still
threaten and frustrate God's purpose. Prayer does not blind us to this
world; it asks God for eyes to see it in the light of God's righteousness in
Christ.

The life that is permitted and required of us—which includes our
social, political, economic life—drives us to prayer, to look to God in Christ,
the author and perfecter of our life; and prayer drives us back to life when it
renews our faith and our reliance on the righteousness of Christ. Prayer is

not some pious duty that stands apart and separated from the other duties of our Christian life; it is an utter necessity *because* of our other duties and the most important resource for the comfort and courage to live as God permits in all our living. Perhaps Calvin said it best: "It remains for us to seek in him, and in prayers to ask of him, what we have learned to be in him" (III, xx, 1).

Toward Honesty in Prayer

It is little wonder, then, that Calvin and the catechism both maintain that prayer must be "from the heart" (Q & A 117). It may not be merely a pious ritual; it may not be merely a mechanical exercise; it may and must be "from the heart." Simply to mouth the words of confession is not to pray; we must honestly "humble ourselves in his majestic presence" (Q & A 117). Simply to let petitions for renewal trip over our lips is not to pray; we must honestly "rest on this unshakable foundation" of God's grace which also claims us. To pray "from the heart," to pray honestly, to feel the hurting sting of our need and misery, and to see the humbling and joyous vision of the life the Lord promises and permits—that is what prayer must be (cf. Q & A 117).

Honesty in prayer has social implications. To pray for the death of the racial lie that plagues ourselves and our society and then continue in our apathy and indifference to the racial situation is not to have prayed "from the heart." To pray regularly and piously for the hungry or the poor and then go on our way unconcerned about the poor in our world and in our communities is not to have prayed "from the heart." Such prayers are more like blasphemy than prayer. And God said, "Even though you make many prayers, I will not listen; your hands are full of blood" (Isa. 1:15). But that exactly is the tragedy of so much Christian prayer—that Christian men and women so seldom bridge the chasm between prayer and practice. It is a kind of schizophrenia that leaves us tragically divided against ourselves.

Not so for the catechism. Prayer is tied to "striving to be renewed more and more after God's image" (Q & A 115). And not so for our faithful Savior, Jesus Christ. When he prayed, "Father, forgive them," he laid down his life for God's fulfillment of that prayer.

When the church of which I am a member first declared a day of prayer for racial reconciliation, they recognized that connection between prayer and work, *ora et labora*: "Members of the Christian Reformed Church, through persevering prayer and the diligent use of their Spirit-given talents, ought to labor unceasingly to cause the light of the gospel of reconciliation to shine upon all men so that the hate engendered in the present racial crisis by the prince of darkness may be speedily dissipated."

Persevering prayer and unceasing labor—that is what praying "from the heart" comes to. The "comfortable" mouthing of phrases of confession (even confession of our social sins) and of petitions for renewal

144

(even the renewal of society) has little to do with the costly comfort of the catechism. Our comfort permits and demands a life of prayer; it gives us the courage for a life of active prayer and prayerful activity—even socially and politically and economically.

In its exposition of the Lord's Prayer, it is worth observing, the catechism adds very little new material. The themes have all been stated before. For example, Qs & As 120 and 121 are closely related to Qs & As 26–28; Qs & As 122–124 are closely related to the material on Christian obedience. Q & A 125 is close to Q & A 27; Q & A 126, to Q & A 56–60; Q & A 127, to Q & A 114. What is new in this section is that the knowledge worked through earlier is turned to petition.

The Christian faith exists as hope and prayer. The norm for belief is the norm for prayer (*lex credendi lex orandi*). The catechism would reject any antithesis between doctrine and piety. And it has been the single point of this book that it would also reject any antithesis between piety or doctrine and engagement in the social and political problems of our life together. Christian faith exists as hope and prayer and as obedience. It is "active in love." The norm for belief is the norm for prayer is the norm for action (*lex credendi lex orandi lex agendi*).

The Social Meaning of the Lord's Prayer

The Lord's Prayer took shape as a protest against the empty phrases and vain repetition with which people try to flatter God and themselves (Matt. 6:7–8). And, indeed, its simplicity and sincerity crystallized the shape of faith as prayer. But its very greatness has made it so familiar that we need to remind ourselves not simply to let the words trip over our tongues. The prayer is committed to memory so easily that we need to will the pause that commits our lives in such prayer. For prayer, too, is not simply a matter of tongue but of life.

When Jesus asked us to say "Our Father," he reminded us of our unity and solidarity. He did not teach us to pray "My Father," as though each of us stood alone. Before God no one stands alone. Before God each person stands related to those near and far, those whom he likes and dislikes, those whom she serves or oppresses. And we "invoke as Father him who judges each one impartially" (1 Pet. 1:17).

Before him we stand with our neighbors in unity and also in equality, for he is no respecter of persons. The master comes to God as one with and equal to the slave when he says "Our Father." The male comes as one with and equal to the female. The white comes as one with and equal to the black. The American comes as one with and equal to the citizen of the Third World. We all clasp hands and approach God together through the Christ in whom there is neither master nor slave, neither male nor female, neither American nor Third-World citizen.

"The childlike awe and trust that God through Christ has become our Father" is "basic to our prayer" (Q & A 120), and it includes our duty to love our brothers and sisters. It is, as Calvin said (3, xx, 38), "For if one father is common to us all, and every good thing that can fall to our lot comes from him, there ought not to be anything separate among us that we are not prepared gladly and wholeheartedly to share with one another." Then "what we ask in faith" (Q & A 120) and what we "expect . . . for body and soul from his almighty power" (Q & A 121) may not be individualistic either, may not be inattentive to the needs of all our neighbors. To quote Calvin again, "All prayers ought . . . to look to that community which our Lord has established in his kingdom and his household" (3, xx, 38). Since that kingdom is a cosmic kingdom, through prayer the believer embraces as brothers and sisters in Christ "not only those whom he at present sees and recognizes as such but all men who dwell on earth" (3, xx, 38).

The petitions that follow the invocation of God as "our Father" express our hope and desire that his future reign will be established soon and already take effect in our lives. Jesus came announcing that kingdom and, in his works and words, made its power felt; and he now sits at God's right hand. Therefore, the petitions "Hallowed be thy name; Thy kingdom come, Thy will be done, on earth as it is in heaven" are said in gratitude for the decisive victory God has won in Jesus Christ even while we "groan inwardly" (Q & A 116) together with the whole creation (Rom. 8:22, 23) for the final unveiling of God's cosmic triumph.

Such petitions nurture lives of humility and confidence and hope (Q & A 117)—lives lived under the sign of the cross, out of the power of the resurrection, and toward the new age of God's peaceable kingdom. Such petitions put us at the disposal of God's name, his "power, wisdom, kindness, justice, mercy, and truth" in "all our living" (Q & A 122). They enlist us against the forces of evil in this world, including injustice and enmity and greed and deceit, until all submit to his rule (Q & A 123). They commit us to obedience, to the costly comfort that receives the permission and command of God with gratitude and "without any back talk" (Q & A 124).

These requests are not otherworldly or individualistic. We are not asking to be rescued from our world or from our communities. Rather, we are asking confidently, hopefully, and humbly that God will reign in our world and in our communities.

Honesty in such a prayer will have significant social effects. If, with these petitions, we yearn for the final consummation of God's victory in Christ, the final destruction of the devil's work, the complete surrender of those principalities and powers that alienate people from God's permissions and from each other, then we must live in yearning too. We must be "straining forward to what lies ahead" (Phil. 3:13), a peaceable kingdom. If we pray in gratitude and in hope for God's victory, then in the interim between resurrection and consummation we must fight the good fight, we must enlist in the battle against human suffering, against hunger and sickness, against war and poverty, against human injustice, against economic inequities and political tyrannies, against racial prejudice and international exploitation. The battle must be joined against "every force" (Q & A 123) which helplessly and hopelessly continues the revolt against God and his intentions with the creation.

That is why the catechism includes the petition "Keep your church strong, and add to it" (Q & A 123). The church serves the kingdom. It yearns for it, and its yearning is its striving against the devil and all his works. Of course, the church knows "His craft and power are great, and armed with cruel hate." It knows "Did we in our own strength confide, our striving would be losing." And therefore it prays. The church knows it cannot itself usher in the new heaven and the new earth; it can only pray for it. But it also knows that Christ has won the victory and "more and more" (Q & A 123) submits to him. It knows there are some things it can and may do which, although they will not themselves usher in the new age, may at least relieve the bitterness of someone's tears, may at least lessen the load of suffering someone carries, may at least make some social relation relatively more just, and which may indeed bring abundant joy and justice to our neighbors. Every member of the church may know that such is "the work he is called to" (Q & A 124).

The next petitions deal with our needs, but without forgetting either God's glory or our neighbor's good. Indeed, they are the bold requests that already, even now in this sad world, God's future and Christ's righteousness may be known and lived, that the heavenly banquet may be already experienced in common bread, that the eschatological joy of forgiveness may be already known in forgiving and being forgiven, and that God's final triumph may strengthen and protect us even now against temptation and evil.

Among these the prayer for daily bread takes first place. In the Bible "bread" is used in two senses—as that which is necessary for life and as an earthly symbol of God's eternal grace. The petition asks God already now for a foretaste of the future manna, of the banquet of his kingdom, but it also asks him to satisfy our physical needs now. Jesus never exalted the soul at the expense of the body. He exalted the whole person. And while the whole person does not live by bread alone, Jesus never belittled the elemental physical needs of people. Neither may we. To pray for a foretaste of the heavenly banquet is to pray for food and nourishment—not just for me, but for *us*, for all those with whom we stand in this petition, with all God's children. Together, in solidarity, we ask for our daily bread. We gather at a common table. There before God shall we habitually take more than our share and leave others hungry?

The catechism reminds us that God is "the only source of everything good" (Q & A 125, cf. Q & A 27) and that nothing God made is god (Q & A 125). The Heidelberg knows that the God who will reign is the creator and provider, and that his care is the world's constant companion (cf. chapter 5). And it reminds us that these affirmations and this petition can only be made in spite of and in the spite of hunger and poverty.

147

The remaining petitions recognize that "in this life even the holiest have only a small beginning of this obedience" (Q & A 114). They ask boldly for the forgiveness of our pasts and deliverance in our futures; and again the petitions are in and for a community. In pleading for our forgiveness, we commit ourselves to forgive our neighbors (Q & A 126). God's permissions do not include being pious toward him while we are merciless toward our neighbors (cf. Matt. 18:21–35). Rather, his permission and our petition are to shape our lives to his forgiveness and righteousness.

The realism of the last petition recognizes that "our striving would be losing" were it not for the power of the one to whom we pray and on whom we rely (Q & A 127). But it is not a request for leave; it is a battle cry. This petition enlists us in just such a world as this one; it enlists us to resist the resistance to God's intentions, to fight the skirmishes, confident that in Christ we "do begin to live according to all, not only some, of God's commandments" (Q & A 114), confident indeed that in Christ we will "finally win the complete victory" (Q & A 127).

We are not honest to God if we pray the Lord's Prayer content to pass through an evil world in safety and "comfort," leaving the world's evil unchallenged. The Lord's Prayer commits us to live in God's costly comfort, loving our neighbor while we are realistic about sin; responsible to God the creator, judge, and redeemer; confessing that God is creator and provider and that Jesus Christ is Lord; sharing in Christ and all his costly benefits; gratefully receiving all God's permissions to live a truly human life.

Prayers for a Social Awakening.

Ordinarily at this point in the chapter we have tried to see the social implications of the catechism with some more specificity. We have tried to follow the catechism's lead into our social lives. In this section the catechism leads to prayer. Its commentaries on the petitions of the Lord's Prayer are themselves prayers. And it seems fitting that we should end our discussion of the catechism, like the catechism itself, in prayers.

Our Father who art in heaven.
We are bold to address you as your son, Christ our Lord, himself has taught us. In our homes we learned to rely on the strength and goodness of our parents. We know how they loved and cared. We know how they suffered to give good things to their children (Q & A 120, Matt. 7:9–11). And your Son has taught us that we may rely still more confidently on your strength and goodness. So we come to you with "childlike awe and trust." It is from you that we "expect everything for body and soul" (Q & A 121, cf. Q & A 26–28). We know that all things are from you and through you. Help us to treat all of your creation as good and nothing of your

creation as god. Help us to live all our life in the certainty of your constant care and in spite of evil.

We come to you, together with all your children, united to them by the grace of your creation and redemption. We thank you for the wonderful variety of races and cultures in your world. Show us your presence even in those most alien to us, until our knowledge of your fatherly love is completed in our love for all our brothers and sisters. Remind us that we invoke as Father him who judges impartially (1 Pet. 1:17). Remind us that we come to you as Father only through Christ, your Son, in whom there is neither rich nor poor, neither male nor female, neither black nor white. And help us strive to be a community "renewed more and more after God's image" (Q & A 115).

Hallowed be thy name.

"Help us to really know you, to bless, worship, and praise you for all your works and for all that shines forth from them: your almighty power, wisdom, kindness, justice, mercy, and truth" (Q & A 122). Help us to live in ways which acknowledge your name, your power and work in our history. Help us to keep free from the blasphemy of piously praying for social, racial, political, economic justice without being willing to make the patient effort necessary to fight injustice. "Help us to direct all our living"— including our living together, "what we think, say, and do"; including our social, racial, political, economic thoughts, words, and deeds—"so that your name will never be blasphemed because of us but always honored and praised" (Q & A 122). Forgive us that some think of you as the rich people's god or the white race's god or the western world's god. Renew us and our social life so that we find and honor your name in our neighbor's good and so that your power, wisdom, kindness, justice, mercy, and truth shine forth from our life together and from our presence in the world. Enlist us in your cause. Refuse our attempts to enlist you in ours. Help us to serve you. Destroy our presumption when we would have you serve us.

Thy kingdom come.

"Rule us by your Word and Spirit in such a way that more and more we submit to you" (Q & A 123). Help us to celebrate your kingship established in Christ and coming in completeness. And even now rule us as a "lover of justice" (Ps. 99:4); even now "judge the world with righteousness, and the peoples with equity" (Ps. 98:9); even now let justice and peace kiss each other and embrace the world (Ps. 85:10). Enable us to celebrate your kingship in the way you permit and require, by submission and obedience to that justice. Enable us under your kingship to be the humble kings who "defend the cause of the poor of the people, give deliverance to the needy, and crush the oppressor" (Ps. 72:4). We give you thanks for the company that acknowledges your kingship and strives for your cause. "Keep your church strong, and add to it" (Q & A 123). Enable her to be the servant of your kingdom, not her own. Through her may your wise kingship "now be made known to the principalities and powers" (Eph. 3:10). Help her to discern your will amid the ambiguities of our social order and help her then to do your will, as the very image of her Lord.

"Destroy the devil's work" (Q & A 123). Destroy the terrible powers of institutionalized oppression and covetousness. Destroy racism and injustice. Destroy corruption and inequity. And permit us to be your instruments of righteousness, your tools of justice. Where there is hatred, make us tools of your love. Where there is injury, make us tools of your healing. Where there is division, make us tools of your unity. Where there is a racial lie, make us tools of your truth. Where there is oppression, make us tools of your deliverance. Wherever there is social evil, make us tools of your righteousness. "Do this until your kingdom is so complete and perfect that in it you are all in all" (Q & A 123).

Thy will be done, on earth as it is in heaven.

"Help us and all men to reject our own wills and to obey your will without any back talk" (Q & A 124). Our only comfort is that we are not our own but belong—body and soul, in life and in death, Sunday and Monday, at worship and at work, politically and economically—to our faithful Savior. Comfort us and give us the courage of our comfort. Command us and give us the grace of your command. "Your will alone is good." Save us from all unwillingness to learn your will, from clinging to our own plans and desires, from trying to limit the scope of your purposes. Save us from cowardice in following your lead, from allowing our ambitions to blur the vision of your will for us, from trying to receive your comfort without the cost. Save us from ignoring the responsibility of our place in your world. "Help everyone carry out the work he is called to as willingly and faithfully as the angels in heaven" (Q & A 124).

We pray that your will may be done in the marketplace, whether the marketplace be international trade or the corner grocery. We pray that your will may be done in assemblies, whether the assembly be the United Nations, the Senate, the City Council, or the Consistory.

Give us this day our daily bread.

Our Father, we stand together in this petition too. We thank you for all your good gifts and for the knowledge that we are all your children. Together then, as if at a common table, we ask for our daily bread. There we confess that some of us habitually take more than our share and leave others hungry. But we dare to pray that you will graciously behold your family and continue to be the provider of every good thing. Save us from misusing your gifts by our greed and selfishness. Save us from indifference to the needs of all your children. Save us from acquiescence in their suffering and hunger. And permit us to glorify you in the stewardship that uses all your gifts for our neighbors' good.

So may we know "that you are the only source of everything good, and that neither our work and worry nor your gifts can do us any good without your blessing" (Q & A 125). Bless us then with food and with your costly blessing so that our participation in Christ may be acknowledged as participation in the one who did not send the hungry multitudes away.

And forgive us our debts, as we also have forgiven our debtors.

"Because of Christ's blood, do not hold against us, poor sinners that we are, any of the sins we do". (Q & A 126). Forgive our sins and help us not to shrink from confession. We would not hide our sins from you, for we believe that you know us as we are and yet you love us. Teach us to respect ourselves for your sake. And permit us so to accept and welcome, to respect and love, to forgive all our neighbors "as evidence of your grace in us" (Q & A 126).

Forgive as well "the evil that constantly clings to us" (Q & A 126), the unrest of the world to which we contribute and in which we share. Forgive the inequities which mark and mar our world but with which we are often aligned and to which we are often indifferent. Forgive the preoccupation with material standards, the discrimination against persons of different color, the indifference to the poor "that constantly clings to us." And forgive us Christians for being so unsure of your comfort that we are unwilling to announce it and to live it and to bear its cost. Forgive us and renew us. Raise us from the paralysis of guilt into "the wholehearted joy in God through Christ" so that we "delight to do every kind of good" (Q & A 90).

And lead us not into temptation, but deliver us from evil.

Father, "by ourselves we are too weak to hold our own even for a moment" (Q & A 127). We do not ask for release from the struggle; we ask for your gracious and demanding presence with us. You have won the victory over the devil, the world, our flesh, the principalities and powers. We pray that we may participate in your victory by your demanding grace. We pray that we may not be tempted to avoid the cost, the cross. Help us to take up his passion, his patient love, and to follow him. Show us the way of the cross. Show us the reality which may shape and reform our social intentions and actions. Show us the reality which may criticize and redefine our political and economic vocations. Show us the reality that enlists us against the pride of power and the sloth of worldly comfort. Show us the power and the comfort of the cross. So "uphold us and make us strong with the strength of your Holy Spirit, so that we may not go down to defeat in this spiritual struggle, but may firmly resist our enemies until we finally win the complete victory" (Q & A 127).

For thine is the kingdom, and the power, and the glory, forever.

"We have made all these requests of you because, as our all-powerful king, you not only want to, but are able to give us all that is good" (Q & A 128). Few of us, Father, are people of very great influence and we wonder sometimes how our prayers can affect society and business and politics. But we know that hunger and oppression and poverty and racism are not the conditions you will for your children. And so we pray to you as the all-powerful king to end them. Father, there are too many children whose lives are handicapped by pain or prejudice, by hatred or boredom, by luxury or poverty, by malnutrition or racism. We know and love some of these. We believe you know and love them all. Take them into the care and skill, the kindness and severity, the love and justice, of your own hands. And help us to be your own hands.

"Your holy name, and not we ourselves, should receive all the praise, forever" (Q & A 128).

Amen.

"This is sure to be! It is even more sure that God listens to my prayer, than that I really desire what I pray for" (Q & A 129). That's the focus of prayer: to say "Amen" to God's intentions, including his social intentions. That's the focus of the catechism: the costly comfort which says "Amen" to God's intentions. May that be the focus of our social life: to say "Amen" to God's intentions.

This book has not tried to say "the last word" about either the catechism or the social message entrusted to the church. It has only intended to be a helpful word, to encourage the churches to think, talk, and pray about their social responsibilities in the light of their confession. But if there must be a last word, then let it be "Amen"—"Amen" to God's intentions for his creation's flourishing.

Acknowledgments and Suggestions for Further Reading

The quotation of Karl Barth at the head of the chapter is from his *The Christian Life* (Grand Rapids: Wm. B. Eerdmans, 1981), pp. 262–263. The book is a profound but difficult treatment of the Lord's Prayer and ethics.

The title of the chapter is indebted to Walter Rauschenbusch, author of *For God and the People: Prayers for the Social Awakening* (Boston: Pilgrim Press, 1910). Rauschenbusch treats the Lord's Prayer and provides wonderful and wonderfully sensitive prayers.

H. Berkhof's "The Catechism as an Expression of Our Faith" and H. Hageman's "The Catechism in Christian Nurture" in Bard Thompson et. al., *Essays on the Heidelberg Catechism* (Philadelphia: United Church Press, 1963) both make some very helpful observations about prayer in the catechism.

Some readers with some experience in biblical studies would find Joachim Jeremias's *The Prayers of Jesus* (London: SCM Press, 1967) a very helpful little book.

Discussion Questions for Chapter 10

1. A possible danger in this chapter is that prayer is being used to accomplish the author's ends rather than God's ends. You might discuss whether the author sufficiently avoids that danger—and whether and how you face the same danger in your prayers.

2. Discuss the Lord's Prayer. The words are so familiar that we seldom really think about what we are saying. Do you agree with the author's interpretation of each petition? To what extent do you accept the author's contention that the Lord's Prayer has much social significance?

3. A doctor was once asked to diagnose a church. She said, "Their prayers suffer from high blood pressure, but their deeds are anemic." What do you suppose she meant by that? Is it true of your church? What would your prescription be?

4. Close in prayer. You could say the Lord's Prayer together. Or you might say the catechism's prayers together, each person reading one petition's prayer. Or class members could take turns saying the prayers in this chapter. Another possibility is to recite a petition of the Lord's Prayer, then pause to allow members of the group to make a request appropriate to that petition. You might be renewed to go and move the world a little. Remember to say "Amen" to God's intentions.